W9-ATE-633

# On Social Welfare

## Other Books by Henry Aaron

*Politics and the Professors: The Great Society in Transition*

*Inflation and the Income Tax* (editor)

*The New View of Property Taxation*

*Why Is Welfare So Hard to Reform?*

*Shelter and Subsidies: Who Benefits from Federal Housing Policies?*

*Social Security: Perspectives for Reform* (with Joseph A. Pechman and Michael K. Taussig)

*Urban Finance and Economic Development: A Case Study of Mexico City* (with Oliver Oldman, Richard Bird, and Stephan Kass)

*Portrait of* Henry Aaron *by Michael Jacques*

# On Social Welfare

## *Henry Aaron*

### Abt Books
#### Cambridge, Massachusetts

**Library of Congress Cataloging in Publication Data**

Aaron, Henry J
  On social welfare.

  "Lectures delivered at Abt Associates and the University of
Michigan during early 1979."
  Includes index.
  1. Social security—United States—Addresses,
essays, lectures.   2. Public welfare—United States—
Addresses, essays, lectures.   3. Insurance, Health—
United States—Addresses, essays, lectures.   I. Title.
HD7125.A18      368.4'3'00973      80-80680
ISBN 0-89011-549-4

© Abt Associates Inc., 1980

All rights reserved. No part of this publication may be re-
produced or transmitted in any form or by any means, elec-
tronic or mechanical, including photocopy, recording, or any
information storage or retrieval system, without specific
permission in writing from the publisher: Abt Books, 55
Wheeler Street, Cambridge, MA 02138.

Printed in the United States of America

368.43
A11

81-1269

# *Contents*

# *Preface*

ANTHONY DOWNS HAS NOTED THE EXISTENCE OF AN "issue-attention" cycle, during which public concern with a problem is born, waxes, reaches a maximum, and then declines. There can be little doubt that the late 1960s and early 1970s represented a high point in the attention accorded to social welfare policy. Not since the Great Depression was the nation so absorbed with the problems of needy groups, the poor in general, minorities, the aged, the poorly housed and fed, and the medically neglected. Whether the advent of the energy crisis, the acceleration of inflation, and the slowdown of real economic growth caused or merely accompanied the decline in passion over these issues, it is clear that the emotion that they once engendered has waned. Part of the reason, no doubt, is that action to aid the needy, embodied in

the flowering of Great Society legislation, increased the real national effort to resolve the
issues, and resulted in a widespread sense that
enough is now being done.

Nevertheless, the fact is that these issues will
not go away. Concern about poverty has given
way to disgust at the partly real and partly imag-
ined "welfare mess." The result is continuing discussion of welfare reform. The political concern
about the aged and poor persons lacking adequate
medical care that gave life to Medicaid and Medicare has been replaced by fear over the terrify-
ingly rapid rise in medical costs and the threat of
financial catastrophe that awaits one subjected to
the blessings of modern, high-technology medicine. The result is the most serious examination of
health insurance by congressional committees
that has occurred in years. The enchantment with
Social Security that led to a 20 percent increase in
benefits in 1972 and to the automatic adjustment
of benefits for inflation has given way to deep
popular concern about the long-term financial viability of Social Security and about the taxes that
must be paid to sustain benefits promised under
current law. But the very trends that give rise to
both of these concerns—the prospect of a large increase in the ratio of retired persons to active
workers during the early twenty-first century and
the simultaneous advent of inflation and slow economic growth—guarantee that the financial problems of the aged will remain front-and-center on
the political stage. Indeed, one can argue that

with the decline of inequality and poverty as national priorities, it will be possible to bring about major reforms in welfare, Social Security, and health protection under the guise of technical improvements in costly elements of the federal budget.

This collection of lectures delivered at Abt Associates and the University of Michigan during early 1979 examined some of the major issues that have to be addressed whenever Congress takes action on welfare, Social Security, or health insurance. They are intended for readers who are interested enough in these problems to consider the serious and sometimes rather technical issues surrounding them. Professional experts in welfare, Social Security, and health insurance should find little that is surprising or new in these lectures, but they may find surprising or annoying the degree to which I have let my sense of political reality interfere with the prescriptions to which they would be led on the basis of hard analysis and ethical presuppositions. If it is a cliché that politics is the art of the possible, then it should be understood that efforts to modify the way we aid the poor, support the aged, and finance health care are as political as any items that each year come before Congress.

Henry Aaron
February 1980

# On Social Welfare

# *1*

# *Social Security*

WHEN FUTURE HISTORIANS REVIEW THE SOCIAL legislation of the first two centuries of American history, they are likely to hail the Social Security Act as the most important single piece of legislation in that entire period, with the possible exception of the Homestead Act. I say this despite the fact that the United States was somewhat laggard among industrial countries in establishing a national program of pensions for the aged, for survivors, and for the disabled. Social Security is now the largest single program in the federal budget. The 1980 budget projected outlays of nearly $116 billion through the Social Security system, $70 billion for the aged alone and another $46 billion for survivors and the disabled. The Social Security budget is also growing very fast. The 1980 budget projected that outlays would rise to about

$141 billion by 1982, assuming enactment of a number of proposals to cut benefits, which the administration submitted with the 1980 budget but which Congress ignored. Because benefits are adjusted automatically for inflation, the jump in prices after the 1980 budget was submitted means outlays will be even higher.

Benefits go to about 35 million Americans each month under the Social Security system, and that number is increasing all the time. The Social Security budget is resistant to the budget-cutting zeal that is apparent in other portions of the non-defense budget. In fact, it grew 5 percent in real terms from 1979 to 1980, and it is virtually guaranteed to grow in real terms every year in the foreseeable future for at least three reasons. First, all benefits currently paid to retirees are automatically adjusted annually for inflation; benefits automatically keep pace with prices. Second, the aged are increasing as a fraction of the population, and until 1976 so were the disabled. The rising proportion of the population on disability insurance was arrested in 1976. Whether this slowdown is temporary or permanent we cannot be sure, but the actuaries are optimistic. Finally, benefits for new retirees increase not only with prices but also with productivity because of the way in which the benefit formula is indexed.

The Social Security system operates basically on a pay-as-you-go basis; that means that annual revenues roughly cover annual benefits, with small variations from year to year as trust funds increase or decrease by relatively modest amounts—modest, that is, in comparison with annual expenditures. Thus, if current benefits rise, taxes have to increase in order to pay for them. A modest trust fund is intended to obviate the need to adjust taxes because of minor economic fluctuations, but the 1975 recession seriously depleted this contingency reserve. Under current law an employee and his or her employer in 1979 had to pay 12.26 percent of the first $25,900 that the employee earned. In 1981 the rate will increase to 13.3 percent and the tax base to $29,700. These increases are a source of great concern to Congress, presumably because they think their constituents do not like them. The onset of recession and the possibility that taxes may have to be cut to fight unemployment have caused some economists to advocate reductions in payroll taxes both to spur the economy and to reduce employers' labor costs (by lowering their payroll taxes).

Despite the size and political impregnability of the Social Security system, it has received considerable criticism lately; its structure and underlying assumptions are being questioned. Many Americans doubt the system's financial viability. Much of the criticism and worry concern the adequacy of legislated taxes to pay for promised benefits. A decade ago the payroll tax was a good deal smaller than it is today, only 9.6 percent of the first $7,800 of earnings; and a decade before that it was nearly invisible, only 6 percent of the first $4,800 of earnings. As recently as 1970 the payroll tax yielded only 44 percent of what the personal income tax yielded. In 1980 it will yield close to two-thirds of what the personal income tax will yield. And if Congress continues its established habit of cutting the personal income tax and increasing the payroll tax, that fraction is likely to grow. If so, the payroll tax could become the largest single tax in the United States sometime late in the twentieth century.

But this trend may well not continue, because resistance to payroll tax increases is growing and interest in putting either general revenues or an earmarked value-added tax into the system also seems to be waxing. Many experts believe that alternatives to payroll tax increases ought to be found. In 1977 the administration proposed a limited use of general revenues to replace the revenues lost to the trust funds due to the excess of unemployment over 6 percent. The last two Advisory Councils on Social Security have suggested using general revenues to pay for the costs of Part A of Medicare. Medicare benefits are not related to earnings; hence, the councils argued, there is little justification for using the payroll tax to pay for it. Others, most notably, the chairmen of the two key committees that handle Social Security legislation, Senator Long and Congressman Ullman, have suggested allocating particular taxes to the Social Security trust fund. Both are enthusiasts of the value-added tax.

A second major question, and one of the two that I want to come back to, is the treatment of the family under Social Security. The Social Security system was designed in 1935, the first taxes collected in 1937, and the first benefits paid in 1940. In 1940 nearly two-thirds of all American households were two-parent families with no earner or only one. Moreover, the divorce rate was considerably below the rate of one divorce for every two marriages that prevails today. By 1977 the fraction of two-parent families with no or one earner had dropped to 34 percent, and the Census Bureau projects that it will drop to about 25 percent by the end of the century. It is interesting, incidentally, that most of the difference is accounted for not by single-parent families with one child, but by increasing numbers of childless individuals. The labor force participation rate of women, both married and single, especially the rate of married women and, even more particularly, of married women with children, has increased dramatically. The changing role of women in the economy and the changing role of the family raise a number of questions concerning the way in which the Social Security system treats the family unit.

Several other questions also deserve attention, some in areas where analysis is sorely lacking at the present time. The first of these concerns the retirement age under Social Security. When the system was initiated, most members of the

labor force (which meant most men) worked beyond the age of sixty-five and spent only a short
period of time in retirement before they died.
Social Security established a retirement age of
sixty-five, which soon became a pattern that private industry and the federal government followed. Then that age began to slip. Benefits were
provided on a reduced basis to retirees down to
age sixty-two, and under some circumstances
down to age sixty. In some private employee pension plans the retirement age is even earlier.
Along with this decline in retirement age longev-
ity is increasing. In the forty years from the incep-
tion of Social Security in 1935 to 1975, life expectancy has increased by about a year and a half for
men and four years for women. It is expected to go
up about another year by the year 2000. Medical
breakthroughs could push it up even more. The
combination of retirement at younger ages and
death at older ages means more years spent in retirement. Is this result of policy and medical
advances a desirable outcome or should the retirement age be increased?

Linked to the retirement age is the retirement
test, the stipulation that benefits are reduced by
the excess of earnings over some basic amount,
now $4,500. It is unquestionably the most un-
popular feature of the system. Each year Congress logs hundreds of proposed bills to do away
with it and to provide benefits to all people at a
particular age, usually sixty-five, irrespective of
subsequent earnings. The reason for these moves

to scrap the retirement test is that most people perceive Social Security as an annuity, not as an earnings replacement system. The founders of Social Security viewed it not only as a system of income, but also as a device for inducing retirement and thereby moving excess labor out of the labor force during the Great Depression; hence, benefits were paid only if people in fact retired. At present most people do not view the system that way. They see it instead as a benefit that they have purchased with payroll taxes and that they should receive at a particular time. The retirement test specifies that benefits are not paid in full if the retiree earns more than $4,500 a year. In 1977 Congress legislated an increase in the amount that people could earn—to a maximum of $6,000 in 1982.

The basic question raised by the retirement age and the retirement test—and the interplay between them—is: should the retirement age be kept at sixty-five, lowered in keeping with retirement policy in a number of occupations, or increased because of longer life expectancy and cost considerations? Another question concerns the retirement test itself: should it be retained or not?

Another issue that has been raised before but is becoming more salient now because of the role of the Supplemental Security Income (SSI) system—welfare for the aged and disabled—concerns the degree to which Social Security should be used as a vehicle for income redistribution. The Social Security system provides people who have low-wage histories or who are married with benefits equal to a larger fraction of average lifetime earnings than the benefits received by people who have high-wage histories or who are single. In this respect, Social Security can be viewed as two systems in one. A proportional replacement rate system gives all workers a return of a bit less than 30 percent of their average earnings during their working lives. On top of that, there is a kind of welfare system that pays something to all beneficiaries except those single workers with the highest covered earnings. The welfare component is proportionately largest for married workers with the lowest lifetime covered earnings. This welfare component advances what traditional supporters of Social Security refer to as the objective of social adequacy. Both the proportional and the welfare components are paid for with a payroll tax proportional to average earnings. This means that single workers and those at the top end of the scale are paying enough in payroll taxes not only to cover their own benefits—their piece of the proportional replacement rate system—but also to pay a piece of the welfare benefits. Until now, the fact that higher income workers have in effect been paying a surcharge to cover this internal redistribution has been obscured by the immaturity of the system, the fact that most current and past retirees receive benefits as if they had worked and paid taxes for their entire working lives, even though they have not done so. Thus, all current retirees and all those about to retire have received a very good rate of return from the Social Security system—much higher than most alternative investments could have yielded.

This situation will not persist indefinitely. The Social Security system has just about matured, in the sense that coverage has been extended to more than 90 percent of the labor force and that the proportion of earnings used in computing benefits and subject to payroll tax is not likely to rise significantly. In a fully mature Social Security system, financed on a pay-as-you-go basis, retirees get a rate of return that is equal to the sum of the rate of population growth and the rate of growth of productivity. This sum tends to be fairly close to the rate of return that people can obtain on alternative investments. On this basis alone, Social Security can continue to be a satisfactory buy, on the average, for each successive cohort. Within each cohort, however, workers with low average earnings and married workers will receive benefits that are larger in relation to their average earnings than will workers with high average earnings. For high earners, especially those who are unmarried, the rate of return on the taxes that they pay and that their employers pay on their behalf will be lower than the rate of return they could receive on alternative investments. In contrast, the rate of return for most married recipients and for all low-income recipients will remain quite high. One should not forget, however, that Social Security provides all workers, high and low earners alike, with kinds of benefits that cannot be

obtained anywhere else; for example, only Social
Security benefits are fully protected against inflation. The value of such unique protection, though
hard to estimate, is surely quite important.

An important question is whether Social Security is an appropriate vehicle to accomplish this
redistribution. Some advocate replacing the current Social Security system with a strictly earnings-related pension and a negative income tax for
the aged. This arrangement would compart-
mentalize all income redistribution in a system
based on need and presumably financed by general revenue; a separate pension system would relate directly to earnings. Many other people want
to retain the present system, arguing that Social
Security is "social insurance"; that is, it merges
the functions of insurance with social objectives,
including some amount of income redistribution.
Still others take an intermediate stand; they argue
that in light of the advent of SSI, the amount of
income redistribution within the Social Security
system should be reduced but not eliminated
entirely.

Another issue, one that dates back to the start
of the Social Security system, is the appropriate relationship between Social Security and private
pensions. Surprisingly, Social Security at first covered only a fraction of the American labor force,
essentially those employed in manufacturing and
large-scale trade. In the 1950s and later coverage
was extended dramatically. But the logic all along
has been that Social Security should provide only

what its advocates have called "the basic floor of protection." The system now covers about 90 percent of all workers. The exceptions are federal employees, some state and local government employees, and a few individuals who work for nonprofit employers. Although 10 percent of workers are not covered at any point in time, nearly everyone will be eligible for Social Security benefits because they will work in Social-Security-covered employment for a long enough period at some time during their lives to become eligible.

Private pensions have also grown enormously, and there are distinct tax advantages associated with them. The employee who wishes to save for retirement is far better off if his or her employer contributes directly to a pension fund on the employee's behalf than if the employer pays the same amount in wages. The former payment is not currently taxable; the latter usually is. Nevertheless, current projections suggest that only about half of the American labor force will be eligible for private pensions when they retire, and the quality of many of these plans is rather poor in several respects. For example, in many occupations if workers are forced to leave their jobs before a stipulated age, they lose all pension rights. In most plans the benefits of employees who shift jobs are poorly protected against inflation even if the right to receive benefits is secured. The Employment Retirement and Security Act (ERISA) is intended to correct the most grievous flaws. There are some rumors to the effect that it may have also slowed the extension of private pension coverage and that a number of small employers have dropped plans to avoid the costs required by ERISA.

Whether or not these rumors are true, the fact remains that roughly half of all workers are unlikely to receive private pensions, and the half who do will get benefits that are not well protected from inflation. Furthermore, their pensions will not be affected by time spent in any job held for too brief a time to be subject to ERISA. In my opinion, the first problem is the most serious one in an inflationary society.

One final issue that has received a good deal of attention lately, primarily because of the work of Martin Feldstein at Harvard, is the question of whether it would be desirable to develop a substantial Social Security trust fund as a device to spur capital formation. Feldstein holds that the U.S. capital stock is suboptimal and favors a variety of devices to increase government savings (or reduce dissavings). He considers the accumulation of a Social Security reserve not only the best instrument at hand, but also a reasonable one, because his work suggests that the availability of Social Security has reduced private saving. Other economists question this evidence and the theory underlying it. While debate over policies to spur capital formation is very much alive, I regard the prospect of using the Social Security trust fund for this purpose at this time as an academic curiosity.

Now let me go back to the question of the treatment of the family. It would be difficult to find a better issue for revealing the complexity of the Social Security system and also the ease with which even the most thoughtful people can embrace inconsistent objectives. I shall also return to the retirement age question, because I think it plays a key role as a profoundly important social policy that is not often recognized as such.

To illustrate the problem of equitable treatment of the family under Social Security, let me draw an analogy to the personal income tax system. There are three objectives in the treatment of the family under the income tax system, each of which sounds reasonable, but which are logically inconsistent. One objective is to make the tax progressive. A second is to treat one- and two-earner families alike, defining like treatment as imposing roughly the same tax when earnings are the same. A third objective is to avoid incentives for or against marriage.

It is simply not possible to achieve all three goals at the same time. Suppose that the same tax is imposed on one- and two-earner families with equal income. Each member of the two-earner family earns half of the income that the single earner does in the one-earner family. Now imagine that all of these earners are single. In that event, the person with the same income as the worker in the single-earner family should pay more than twice the tax of the earners with the same incomes as the members of the two-earner family, if the tax system is to be progressive. But this creates either a marriage incentive or disincentive.

In the case of Social Security there is a similar inconsistency among four objectives that are commonly articulated with respect to the treatment of the family. The first objective is to make benefits that are triggered when earnings are lost because of retirement, disability, or death a function of the earnings loss. Second, the system should not encourage divorce. Third, the system should treat one- and two-earner families alike. Related to the third goal is the principle (stated vaguely and in somewhat different ways by different people) that marriage should be treated as an economic partnership, or, taking a somewhat different viewpoint, the system should recognize unpaid work done in the home.

All of those goals sound worthwhile, but they are difficult to reconcile. Under the present system each spouse receives either a benefit based on his or her own earnings history or a "dependent" spouse's benefit equal to half of the benefit to which the sole or principal earner is entitled, whichever is larger. The dependent spouse's benefit is always larger than the worker's own benefit if the spouse earned less than one-sixth of the family's combined earnings. The worker's benefit is always greater than the dependent spouse's benefit if the spouse earned more than one-third of the combined family earnings. In the typical case, where the wife earns a minor fraction of combined family earnings, she receives no reward for the taxes she has paid if she earns less than one-sixth of the family's combined earnings—the dependent spouse's benefit is greater. And if she earns more, she receives the excess of the benefit based on her own earnings history over the dependent spouse's benefit as reward for the taxes she has paid. She is also eligible for disability benefits and her survivors may be eligible for benefits if she dies, but those benefits do not compensate for the taxes she pays. Thus, because a nonworking spouse gets a dependent's benefit "for free," the extra benefits a working wife receives because she has worked are much smaller in relation to the taxes she pays than are her husband's. Exactly the same provisions apply to men and exactly the same problem arises if they are the lesser earner, but this situation is relatively uncommon. A corollary of this problem is that one-earner couples get larger benefits in relation to taxes paid than do two-earner couples. In fact, one-earner couples receive larger benefits on a given earnings history than do two-earner families with the same combined earnings. It could be argued that there is some justification for this differential because in economic terms a one-earner couple with the same income as a two-earner couple has a higher standard of living. There is more nonmarket work time available to that family, and hence their living standard should be higher. However, this argument carries weight only with an economist. The general opinion seems to be that one- and two-earner families with the same earnings history should get the same benefit.

Still other problems arise in the case of divorce. A divorced homemaker married for fewer than ten years is not entitled to any benefits based on her former spouse's earnings record. If the marriage lasted at least ten years, she is entitled to retirement benefits equal to half of those which her divorced spouse receives on his entire earnings history, but she gets those benefits only when and if he retires. If she is older than her former spouse or he works past retirement age, she may be eligible for no benefit on his record until she is well past the age of sixty-five. Basing eligibility on the retirement of a former spouse a woman may not have seen for decades is quite ridiculous.

The problems just described are "real" problems—real in the sense that they involve differences in benefits that many regard as unfair. But perhaps the most important criticism made of the present system is a symbolic one—that women should not be regarded as dependents or adjuncts under the Social Security system. It is argued that women should receive benefits in their own right, not as a result of something their spouses did. I do not think that any proposed solution to the treatment of women will be acceptable to many women's organizations unless this problem is dealt with.

A second necessary element of any program to reform the way women are regarded under Social Security is provision of some reward for earnings from the first dollar of earnings. The secondary earner should not have to earn enough to provide a benefit equal to at least 50 percent of the spouse's benefit in order to increase the family's benefits.

A third element must be some improvement in the treatment of homemakers and divorced people. Consider the typical case of a woman who withdraws from the labor force shortly after marriage to bear children and who remains out of the labor force for an extended period of time. She eventually loses eligibility for disability insurance, if she ever had it. If the marriage terminates, she will not be eligible for any kind of benefit based on her husband's record unless the marriage has lasted ten years. Even if she goes back into the labor force at that point, her lack of earnings during the years when she was out of the labor force will reduce the benefit that she can earn in her own right in later years.

Three major solutions for these problems have been advanced. One is earnings sharing, under which each spouse would receive credit for half of the couple's combined earnings. By itself, this proposal suffers from fatal shortcomings, although it does express the idea that marriage is an economic partnership to which each spouse contributes. It would permit the repeal of dependent's benefits for spouses and would entitle survivors to benefits in their own rights. The flaws derive from the fact that benefits for many classes of beneficiaries would be drastically reduced, notably for widows of husbands who were the sole or principal earner. At present such widows receive benefits based on their husband's full earnings; under earnings sharing, benefits would be based on only half. Principal or sole earners who became disabled would receive benefits on only half of their own earnings rather than on their full earnings, as under present law. To deal with these two solutions, the Department of Health, Education, and Welfare's (HEW) Women's Report and the Report of the 1979 Advisory Council on Social Security both propose two modifications to earnings sharing. Earnings would be split when computing benefits only if it would help the couple, relative to present law. In addition, widows and widowers would inherit part or all of their deceased spouse's earnings history.

With these modifications, the principal gainers from earnings sharing are spouses, usually wives, who at present do not have eligibility for disability insurance during periods when they are out of the labor force, but would acquire such eligibility under earnings sharing. The principal losers are divorced men, who lose half of their own earnings history and acquire half of the usually much smaller earnings of their spouse. A lengthy transition provision could soften the impact of these changes on men.

Earnings sharing has many attractions. But it is expensive, principally because of disability benefits for homemakers. While such a liberalization has some appeal, it is not the most important potential use of public funds. Disabled homemakers can count on the earnings of a spouse for support. At the same time millions of Social Security recipients remain in poverty because of low benefits. Furthermore, the reductions in benefits for divorced men may not be acceptable to many people, mostly to men. For these reasons, a more modest set of changes has some appeal. Under this restricted approach, earnings would be shared at divorce, but only for retirement benefits, and surviving spouses would inherit their deceased spouse's earnings history. This pair of proposals would assure all aged divorced women and surviving widows old-age benefits in their own right, but would continue the wife's benefits for intact couples. Married women could be assured old-age benefits in their own right if, in addition to earnings sharing at divorce and inheritance of earnings, the earnings history of both spouses of an intact marriage were averaged before old-age benefits were computed.

A second plan would provide "earnings" credits for homemakers. This approach raises several serious definitional and judgmental questions. For example, what wage rate would be applied in the case of the homemaker? How would we finance the homemaker credit? If we impose a payroll tax on the family, should it be compulsory or voluntary? If voluntary, each family would face a complex and possibly divisive decision each year. If dependent spouse's benefits were retained, homemaker credits would be a very bad buy, and nobody would want them. Even if dependent spouse's benefits were abolished, many families might elect not to buy homemaker coverage. If benefits were needed at a later time, what could be done about them? If such a tax were compulsory, the burden on low-income families might far exceed the value of potential benefits in the eyes of those whom the proposal is intended to help. If homemaker credits were financed from general revenues, how would we establish equity among part-time workers, volunteers, and nonhomemakers? All in all, this approach appears to raise more problems than we know how to solve.

The third solution is the most radical by far, and that is probably its fatal flaw. This plan would convert Social Security into a double-deck system. The first deck would be a flat grant for all the aged and the disabled, paid on the basis of citizenship, irrespective of any prior earnings history or payroll taxes. The second deck would be a pension that is strictly proportional to earnings. This plan would resolve most of the family problems and women's complaints about the system. Every member of society, including those who had never been employed, would receive the first-deck benefit. It is possible to structure the system so that in both decks changes in benefit levels for most classes of recipients would be relatively small, and the various problems mentioned above could be avoided. The dependent spouse's benefit would be entirely eliminated.

The problem with this approach—one that I think will make it politically unacceptable—is in the first deck. How would we pay for it? And would it really be universally available? Supporters of Social Security, including organized labor and most old-age groups, fear that the first deck, paid for by general revenues, would become means-tested. They feel that means tests degrade recipients and should be used as little as possible.

I feel such a fear is exaggerated even if the universal grant is paid for with general revenues and that it has no substance if it is paid for by a special surtax or an earmarked portion of the income tax. Economists typically deplore such financial legerdemain, but I feel it may play a constructive role with respect to the long-term commitments entailed in Social Security by cementing social support of those commitments.

Many people agree that if one can avoid that risk, there is a great deal to be said for this kind of double-deck system. It resolves the family problems almost completely. As a by-product, it also solves the problem of universal coverage that is now bedeviling Congress—the issue of how and under what terms Social Security should be extended to all people not now covered.

Another aspect of Social Security policy that has begun to undergo reexamination is the appropriate age at which benefits should be paid. At first retirement benefits were paid at age sixty-five. First women and then men were later provided reduced benefits as early as age sixty-two if they wanted to receive benefits before sixty-five.

It is clear that in the last forty years there has been a trend toward earlier retirement. One can interpret this trend in two completely different ways. The first emphasizes the major increase in personal income during the first half of the twentieth century, and notably since the Great Depression. Leisure is what economists call a normal good—one that people consume in increasing amounts as income rises; it may even be a superior good—one whose consumption rises more than proportionately with income. As income has risen, one would expect people to wish to consume more leisure. Early retirement is one way to do so. According to this interpretation, Social Security has followed rather than shaped the trend toward early retirement. It has simply ratified and perhaps systematized a trend that would otherwise have varied across the population. The second interpretation turns the first on its head by asserting that, although rising income has increased the public's taste for leisure, Social Security has been an independent and very potent force in reducing the age of retirement.

It would be rather interesting to know which of these hypotheses is correct. At the present time we simply do not know which is nearer the truth. There are snippets of information that suggest that the second is nearer to the truth than the first. When various changes have been made in the Social Security system, such as the introduction of provisions to provide benefits for retirement before the age of sixty-five, there has been a noticeable shift in retirement behavior. However, a supporter of the first interpretation could argue that these shifts merely occur a bit ahead of time and would have happened in any event.

The age at which workers normally retire has an important bearing on the cost of Social Security for active workers. The earlier the retirement age, the larger is the population of retirees and the smaller is the population of active workers paying taxes to support retirement benefits. In a Social Security system that operates on a pay-as-you-go basis the tax rate—the proportion of earnings that the active labor force has to pay in taxes—is equal to the product of two ratios. One is the number of beneficiaries to the number of active workers. The other is the ratio of the average benefit to the average taxable wage. The product of these two ratios is the tax rate necessary to sustain retirement and disability benefits. Over the next half century the first of these ratios will increase 50 percent; that means that, other things being equal, the cost of Social Security in pay-as-you-go terms will go up about 50 percent, if the ratio of benefits to average covered earnings stays the same. Of course, a sharp and unexpected increase in birth rates could prevent some of this increase in costs from occurring. An unexpected jump in labor force participation among the aged would lower costs. A greater than anticipated increase in life expectancy would drive up costs more than current forecasts project.

The upcoming rise in the ratio of retirees to active workers means that over the next few decades some very important decisions must be made. I think that decisions concerning the retirement age will have to be made within the next ten years, because the political power of the aged after that time will make it virtually impossible to increase the retirement age. The aged vote more often than the rest of the adult population. In the future close to a majority of the voting-age population will be getting retirement or disability benefits or will be within five to ten years of retirement. Furthermore, any increase in the retirement age should be legislated many years before it becomes effective to provide people time to adjust their plans.

The importance of the issue is heightened by the possibility that, to paraphrase the Surgeon General, retirement "may be dangerous for your health." There is some evidence that continuation of work is healthful and that the trend toward earlier retirement may cause physical problems. The evidence is weak because the causal relationship is unclear. People may retire—and in fact there is a lot of reason to think they *do* retire—because of ill health. Even so, psychological and medical evidence suggests that retirement is not healthful—at least retirement as it is commonly practiced in the United States. It may be that forced retirement is harmful, but voluntary retirement is not. In any case, however, the choice of retirement age has important implications for the cost of Social Security and is likely to grow in importance as demographic trends drive up costs. It is an area we know very little about at the present time, but research, possibly even some social experimentation, may have something to teach us. And before that demographic wave washes over us, we do have the time to act on the results of such research.

In conclusion, Social Security appears to be at a watershed. It has just about reached maturity, as that term is used by actuaries. We are facing demographic trends that portend major increases in costs early in the twenty-first century. Right now we lack the information required to know how to respond to them, but the unique feature of this crisis is that its shadow is clearly visible sufficiently far in advance for us to do the necessary research and act upon it.

**Question:** Workers enjoy a high rate of return on their own payroll taxes, do they not?

**Aaron:** Yes. The question is, what happens to the employer's contribution? Economists have argued about it for forty years. It is clear that over the long haul the employer's payroll tax is not a profits tax. Therefore, either it is reflected in product prices and hence is borne in proportion to consumption, or it is reflected in lower wages. Although the mechanism is in some dispute, most economists accept the second hypothesis; that is, over the not so very long haul, the employer's contribution is reflected in lower real wages. I think this view is compelling. Employers should not care, in computing the labor costs they are prepared to incur, whether they pay a dollar in payroll taxes or a dollar in wages.

**Question:** What do we know about people's desires for postretirement benefits and their preretirement willingness to pay taxes? Much of your discussion seems to assume a kind of theoretical economic equity that may or may not reflect the actual need for income and reduced taxes on the part of the individuals involved.

**Aaron:**   There's a good deal of information available on what people are actually receiving and on the economic status of various groups among the aged. We know that the older aged are financially far worse off than the younger aged, for a variety of reasons. They were poorer when they retired than were the younger retired, and inflation has eroded the real value of any private pensions to which they may have been entitled. They have used up some or all of any other assets that they may have accumulated. We know that widows are poorer than widowers, and both are poorer than couples. The reasons in this case are more complicated. There's probably some confounding of the effects of age in these statistics as well, but even adjusted for age, couples are still better off. It's not quite clear why. Perhaps both members of the couple were reasonably healthy and had a greater capacity to earn before retirement. It is clear that single males do not do as well at any stage in life as married males; they neither live as long nor earn as much.

As for what people want, I'm not sure we really know, nor am I confident that we would find out by asking them. What people want in regard to retirement involves decisions that will affect them far into the future. The basic justification for mandatory Social Security, and indeed the basic justification for most contractual savings plans, is that people are not rational in their voluntary savings behavior for retirement.

**Comment:** They do not know what they want, or they may want things that others believe are bad for them.

**Aaron:** I'll accept your reformulation. But there is also a problem of moral hazard in that we bank on some kind of safety net for the aged. As a nation we have made clear that aid will be given to the destitute and that the conditions of such aid will not be utterly demeaning. Therefore, there is a problem of moral hazard in that the first few dollars we save are really worthless in terms of the net addition that they're going to make to our retirement behavior. Enough people may be affected by that information to provide one reason for a mandatory retirement system. We do not really know, except through the electoral process, what people want, and I am not confident we could find out through alternative means.

**Question:** Are there any patterns of racial or demographic differences in terms of benefits received?

**Aaron:** A few years ago Milton Friedman speculated that certain characteristics of Social Security tend to operate against blacks and other minorities, the poor, and the poorly educated. Minorities enter the labor force early because they drop out of school early, so they pay taxes for a longer period of time. But they also die younger. I did some research on these speculations and concluded that the progressive elements within the system were sufficient to balance the fact that low-income groups work longer and die younger. I did the paper largely to provoke thorough investigation of the question by the Social Security Administration. They did a series of studies which pointed out that minorities are disproportionate recipients of disability and survivor benefits. Together with the progressive elements of the benefit formula, these features are sufficient to override the effects on minorities of early entry into the labor force and premature death, and the system still remains a satisfactory buy for all groups.

**Question:** Did they do the studies themselves or did they commission them?

**Aaron:** They did them themselves.

**Comment:** They generally tend to conclude that papers containing adverse conclusions are wrong.

**Aaron:** The fact that they concluded as they did does not prove that the adverse conclusions are right.

**Question:** You talked about possible reforms. What would you do, given your current state of knowledge, to reform the system? If you were to conduct more research, what kind of research would you do? How much of the research we need to do did you get started when you were at HEW?

**Aaron:** That's an embarrassing question, but I'll answer it. First, as to what changes ought to be made, I think the issue of the double-deck system should be ventilated in public. Academics have considered it, other countries have had variations on the theme, but it has not received sufficient visibility or consideration in the United States to become part of the political dialogue. Now it may well be that the risk of means testing a large part of the system is sufficient to render that option unattractive. Some people would welcome this "risk," but I would not like to see a drastic increase in means testing. Still, the double-deck idea deserves to be ventilated. The family and women's issues in Social Security are probably the most important structural issues now confronting the system. With respect to the retirement age, it seems to me that cost precludes any reduction in age; the operative questions are whether, and if so how, the retirement age should be increased. Any proposal simply to raise the age at which full benefits are paid would be highly controversial. It would require extensive discussion before any elected official would be willing to consider it.

When I was at HEW, we kept saying how important it was to do research on the aged, but none of us had much time to spend on research. There is a kind of Gresham's Law of government agencies. Immediate problems drive out long-term planning and research. Under an activist HEW secretary immediate problems were available in abundance. One of the issues that I think needs attention is the retirement age. There should be research on the role of private pensions—the process by which people acquire assets and prepare financially and psychologically for retirement. We also need to have more information on the aging process following retirement. The vistas of ignorance are almost boundless and one of the major goals should be to identify what data we have, what data we could get, and what the best research methods would be for dealing with these questions.

**Question:** Do you have any idea how many people receiving Social Security benefits today have small enough benefits that they qualify for SSI?

**Aaron:** About 2 million. There are another 2 million people on SSI who are disabled.

**Question:** Wouldn't the double-decker be substantially more expensive than the current package, or why wouldn't it be, if essentially the current package is means tested?

**Aaron:** It need not be substantially more expensive. The reason it would not be expensive is that one way or another most people are getting that first deck of benefits through either Social Security or SSI. Perhaps a few wealthy people who are not eligible for SSI or Social Security would get first-deck benefits, but the cost would be small. Although there are differences in the way in which entitlement is acquired and the computation is done when the benefit-triggering event occurs, the pattern of benefits would not be radically different for most classes of beneficiaries from that under current law. One way to make it a lot cheaper is to index the first deck by prices. As one of the Rothschilds once said, "Compound interest is the eighth wonder of the world." It turns out that the difference between wage indexing and price indexing—which is just productivity growth over time—has an enormous impact, spread over forty or fifty years, on the cost of the system. Price indexing the first deck is tantamount to price indexing the entire system, because the only place it really matters is on that first deck. Whether the second deck is indexed by prices or wages turns out not to matter.

**Question:** So we would continue to wage index that part?

**Aaron:** We could wage index it or price index it. If we price indexed the first deck and made no further changes, the cost of the system would diminish markedly over time. As a practical matter, Congress would liberalize the system on a discretionary basis in even-numbered years, as they did in the 1950s and 1960s.

**Question:** You pointed out that problems in the treatment of the family under Social Security are analogous to problems under the income tax. How could you deal with the latter problems?

**Aaron:**   The marriage disincentive problem is receiving considerable attention at the present time. One solution would be to shift to a genuine individual income tax. Another would be to provide some kind of credit for second earners. Each of these approaches would solve the problem or substantially reduce it. As a by-product, incidentally, we would stop treating one- and two-earner families alike, but that concern seems to be diminishing. Our treatment of one- and two-earner families developed as a result of community property laws that proliferated in a number of states immediately after World War II. The federal government did not want to, did not know how to, or did not know it could override these community property laws. So we sort of backed into our system of income splitting. It prevailed for a long period of time and created enormous marriage incentives.

**Comment:**   Now there are enormous marriage disincentives. According to a paper by Munnel on marriage, the present value for a high-income family with earnings equally divided approaches $100,000.

**Aaron:**   You would need two $50,000 earners to have that kind of situation, and those are exceptional cases. In fact, one $100,000 earner can end up splitting income through a marriage settlement.

**Question:** You talked about splitting income for purposes of Social Security benefits and benefit-triggering mechanisms?

**Aaron:** There are two alternative ways of handling it. Either we can have an individual wage base for each worker, as we do under current law, or we can establish a wage base for the combined earnings of couples, in which case we could rebate excess tax payments on earnings over the couple's base in the same way that under current law excess tax payments on earnings over the individual's wage base are rebated if an individual works for two or more employers and has earnings over the wage base. Essentially, those are the two alternatives. Logically, the couple's base makes more sense.

There's an important negative aspect of earnings splitting that I did not mention. In the event of divorce, the earner from a one-earner family will receive a benefit based on half his or her earnings. Although women's groups are not likely to quarrel with that result, many workers view their earnings histories as their own; they do not see marriage as a partnership in that sense.

**Question:** What about double dipping by government employees? Do you think universal coverage is an interesting reform that might be made?

**Aaron:** I think it might be worth describing what the problem is. There would be no problem if Social Security had a proportional benefit formula, that is, if benefits were proportional to average earnings. Consider an individual who has worked for ten years in the Social Security system and thirty years in another system. His or her average earnings for Social Security will eventually be computed over a thirty-five year period, and the benefit will be based on average earnings. The replacement rate will be the same as that of a worker who has spent thirty-five years under the Social Security system and earned a wage ten-thirty-fifths as large as the first worker. The benefit formula provides a higher replacement rate for workers with low average earnings than for workers with high average earnings. As far as the benefit formula is concerned, there is no difference between a low-wage earner and a high-salaried civil servant who leaves the government at age fifty-five and works for ten years at the maximum under Social Security if total earnings covered by the payroll tax are the same for the two individuals. The civil servant will look poor in terms of the benefit formula and hence will receive a very high replacement rate.

There are two basic ways to deal with the double-dipping problem. One is to bring presently exempt employees immediately or gradually into the Social Security system; the other pension systems to which they now belong would be converted to a second tier on top of Social Security. About 30 percent of all state and local employees are not covered by Social Security. No permanent federal employees are covered, except military personnel, who are covered by both military pensions and Social Security. The other approach would be to reduce Social Security benefits for employees whose earnings are low because they worked in uncovered employment. The first approach is superior because it would close certain gaps in protection for workers who move between covered and uncovered employment. The transition must be gradual if the first course is adopted, particularly for state and local government employees.

**Question:** Why is that the case?

**Aaron:** Essentially, in many plans—such as that in Massachusetts, at least until very recently—all of the payments that are currently being made by the state and by the worker pay for current retirees. Those payments have to continue to be made. If state employees are brought into the Social Security system, there will be the additional Social Security payroll tax, which could create severe fiscal and political problems. For this reason I think it would be difficult to bring all state and local employees under Social Security in one grand reform. It may well be possible, however, to cover all new employees under Social Security and give previously hired employees the option of retaining present coverage or of moving under Social Security with a new state or local pension as a supplement.

The second way of dealing with the problem is less direct, but in the long run it would be almost as effective in eliminating the windfall benefits short-service workers now enjoy. Indeed, over the

long run it might make possible the first
approach. This second approach would be to
change the way in which the basic benefit is calculated under Social Security. There are at least two
ways to do this. One way is to calculate the benefit
based on the worker's total earnings, covered and
uncovered, but give the person a proportion of
that benefit equal to the ratio of covered earnings
to total earnings, covered and uncovered. Another
and less generous way is to calculate a Social
Security benefit both on all earnings, covered and
uncovered, and on uncovered earnings only. The
actual Social Security benefit would equal the difference. This is the less generous method because
in effect it provides Social Security benefits at
very low rates for relatively high-wage workers on
their last few dollars of earnings. I have no idea
which, if either, of these methods Congress would
choose.

**Comment:** You mentioned earlier that the
ratio of Social Security tax revenues to general
revenue is increasing.

**Aaron:** That's right.

**Comment:** That suggests that to some extent general revenues should be used for Social
Security because the payroll tax is not as good an
automatic stabilizer as the personal or corporation
income tax. It also suggests that Social Security
funds could be used as an instrument of fiscal policy. Has that ever been considered?

**Aaron:** There are two ways in which the personal income tax is useful as a fiscal policy instrument. One is as an automatic stabilizer and the other is as a discretionary instrument. If the personal income tax declines as a portion of total revenues, its power as an automatic stabilizer will tend to decrease, other things being equal. If elasticity increases because the rate structure shifts, the value of the income tax as an automatic stabilizer could continue. From the standpoint of discretionary policy, it is not clear to me that a tax instrument yielding about 50 percent of total revenues is that much weaker than one that is yielding a somewhat larger fraction. In fact, the proportion of revenues from the personal income tax has not changed much, because the decline of the corporation income tax as a proportion of federal revenues has just about offset the payroll tax increase.

Payroll taxes have already been used as a fiscal policy instrument. For years the precise timing of payroll tax increases has been influenced by economic considerations. Congress on a number of occasions has stretched out or slowed down payroll tax increases for fiscal reasons. The important issue—the one the 1980 budget raised—is what happens when the expenditure side of Social Security begins to be used as a fiscal policy device. With Social Security accounting for $115 billion of the 1980 budget, it is very hard to ignore. In fact, in 1979 a number of benefit reductions were proposed, to be effective in 1980, that would have saved just under $1 billion in 1980 but far more in the future. I think one of the reasons that there was so much political controversy over the administration's Social Security proposal in the 1980 budget was that the expenditure side of the program has not previously been considered a fiscal policy instrument.

**Question:** Can that be skirted if, for example, expenditure is used only as an expansionary instrument and the actual payroll tax is used as a contractionary one?

**Aaron:** We are already faced with large increases in payroll taxes. Starting some time in the 1980s, we are going to move into a period when the trust fund will grow quite rapidly under current law. On the other hand, given current expenditure projections, the payroll tax cannot be cut before 1981, and perhaps not even then, because there isn't enough money in the trust fund. If a large and protracted recession had begun in 1979, the Social Security trust fund would have been in trouble, and we would have had to consider either putting general revenues into it before the 1981 tax increase or legislating an increase in taxes into 1980. My guess is that the former solution would be chosen, despite the great reluctance of Congress to allow the use of general revenues for Social Security.

**Question:** What is the status of the idea of putting disability and health payments into general revenues and reducing the Social Security tax so that it covers only retirement?

**Aaron:** The last two Advisory Councils supported paying for Medicare from general revenues. However, there does not seem to be any interest in paying for disability benefits from general revenues.

**Question:** Why not?

**Aaron:** Because it is an earnings-related benefit, as is retirement, whereas Medicare is not.

**Question:** Are there any estimates of how private employers are attempting to modify their own pension planning to compensate for the weaknesses of the government system and to take advantage of its strengths?

**Aaron:** I don't know what employers with private pension plans are doing. But they would be better advised to worry about how to manage private pensions in an inflationary environment than to be concerned about the Social Security system, which is fundamentally sound. Inflation seriously erodes the value of pensions once they are claimed and undercuts the value of entitlements of employees who shift jobs.

**Comment:** It seems to me that all of these uncertainties make for increasing costs for both private and public insurers.

**Aaron:** Those who were disturbed about the 1980 budget proposal argued that we sacrifice something very important and very fragile when we begin to tamper with the benefit structure. At present, most people count on Social Security; they know what they are going to get. If a lot of changes are introduced, even relatively minor ones, such as those proposed by the administration that year, the people's confidence in the system may be jeopardized.

On the other hand, Social Security benefits are too large and growing too fast to be regarded as sacrosanct. They need to be modified as our priorities change. The key is to give beneficiaries an assurance that their benefits will not be cut and to give workers ample warning before the structure of benefits is changed.

**Question:** Is there perhaps a hidden purpose in trying to destroy the system in order to increase the private savings rate for capital formation?

**Aaron:** Not at all. The real motive was the openly acknowledged one of trying to shift expenditures from low-priority uses to high-priority uses.

**Question:** Is there any research on the relationship between health insurance for the aged (including nursing homes) and Social Security benefits? The main expenses of aged retirees are likely to be medical, so these two systems are highly interactive.

**Aaron:** Well, nursing homes cost more than hospitals now through Medicaid.

**Question:** I know, but I'm thinking of the middle-class folks who do not want to be dependent on Medicaid for all of their health and benefits after they retire. How do private pension plans, as a source of income for financing personally selected medical care, compare with Social Security financing? What about the availability of health insurance for the aged? Medical expenditures are the main drain on the income of the aged; to determine need and the preferred or reasonable level of benefit, we have to consider the extent to which such expenditures are covered.

**Aaron:** You raise some very important questions. I do not know the answers. We need to look at who is getting what, cross-tabulate this information, and see how it is changing over time.

**Question:** Do we know whether we want people to work beyond retirement age? Does our government have an explicit policy on retirement?

**Aaron:** Our government has several different policies which are mutually inconsistent. It prohibits mandatory retirement and encourages retirement through pension programs. Moreover, the pension programs have the effect of encouraging private institutions to make retirement all but mandatory.

*2*

# *Welfare Reform*

45

THE FIRST THING THAT I WOULD LIKE TO DO IS INDI-
cate the dimensions of the subject of welfare reform. Then I'll turn to some of the problems with
the existing system, note the dilemmas posed by
various solutions, and offer a few lessons from the
welfare reform debate of the past two years.
Finally, I'll allude briefly to some radical alternatives which I do not think are likely to be enacted
but which are nevertheless based on interesting
arguments.

## THE DIMENSIONS OF WELFARE REFORM

The definition of welfare reform is in the eye of the
beholder. How one defines the boundaries to some
extent indicates one's view of what welfare is and
what it should be. Nobody would suggest that

welfare does not include income-tested programs
that provide cash without restrictions as to how it
will be spent. A major program in this category is
Aid to Families with Dependent Children (AFDC),
which provides state and federal funds for indigent single parents with dependent children.
Another program that is always included is Supplemental Security Income (SSI), which provides
assistance for the aged, blind, and disabled. It is
the one piece of President Nixon's family assistance plan that was passed. In 1977 expenditures
under these two programs totaled almost $17 bil-
lion, somewhat more than two-thirds by the federal government and the rest by states and locali-
ties. Neither share has risen very much in nominal
dollars since 1977 and both have declined in real
terms and as a fraction of the gross national product (GNP). In fact, looking at AFDC and SSI together, in 1980 they are going to claim smaller
fractions of GNP than in any year since 1973. One
reason is that the economic recovery from the
1974–1975 recession has somewhat reduced the
client population in some areas and slowed its rate
of increase in others. The second reason is that the
states have not been adjusting standards of need
and payments to keep up with inflation, so that
real benefits have tended to decline. General
Assistance, a collection of state and local programs, directed over $1 billion in 1977 to needy
people not covered by AFDC and SSI. The bulk of
General Assistance is provided by New York and
California, two states that have been under fiscal
constraints for quite different reasons.

In addition to AFDC, SSI, and General Assistance, other programs provide assistance with a variety of restrictions. Since 1977, food stamps have been offered under such unrestrictive terms that they are almost equivalent to cash. Before 1977 households bought a certain quantity of food stamps based on family size for a certain outlay (the purchase requirement) based on family size and net income. The difference between these amounts is the "bonus value." In 1977 Congress decided to give eligible families the bonus value without any purchase requirement. These amendments made it easier for officials to administer the program and easier for potentially eligible families to claim benefits. Because the bonus value is now provided upon application and is less than most families spend on food, food stamps are essentially equivalent to cash, except that food stamps, unlike cash, may carry some stigma.

Arguably, Veteran's Pensions for disabilities not connected with prior military service belong in any discussion of welfare reform. Unlike Veteran's Compensation, which is only for service-connected injuries, about half of the Veteran's Pensions are paid to veterans over the age of sixty-five purely because of low income, which is regarded as prima facie evidence of disability. Thus, at least half of the program is simply a separate welfare program for the aged, one which is now considerably more generous than any of the other programs I've noted so far.

A third program that should be included in any welfare reform discussion is the Earned In-

come Tax Credit. This program is structured
rather differently from the others. Instead of
guaranteeing a fixed amount of assistance, it provides a supplement of up to $500 on earnings of up
to $5,000. The amount of the supplement is re-
duced for income in excess of $6,000 and vanishes
at $10,000.

All of these programs except Veteran's Pensions have been included in the welfare reform discussion since 1977. Various other programs have
not been included in these discussions, usually because the income-tested aid they provide is tied to
particular commodities. The prominent examples
are Medicaid, Housing Assistance, Basic Educa-
tional Opportunity Grants, and social services
that are provided on an income-tested basis. Beyond simply assisting recipients to increase their
general purchasing power, these programs attempt to specify what types of purchases should
be made. All of these programs express a kind of
commodity egalitarianism. In other words, the
objective is not to equalize income but to equalize
consumption of certain commodities regarded as
necessary, such as health care or housing, or
regarded as meritorious, such as education. The
one restricted form of assistance included in the
welfare reform debate since 1977 is Public Service
Employment, which provides income assistance
on the condition that beneficiaries work.

Another group of programs is also excluded
from the welfare reform discussion notwithstand-
ing the fact that collectively the assistance they
provide to low-income people is far more important than that of the programs I've noted. This

group includes Social Security, Medicare, Railroad Retirement, Black Lung, Disability Insurance, and Unemployment Insurance. All are entitlement programs; some of them have quasi-income tests (for example, Social Security has an earnings rather than an income test). These programs provide enormous transfers to the low-income population but their objectives are broader. Payments are made as a matter of right to recipients who meet certain conditions other than low income. The fact that these conditions are correlated with low income is very important from the standpoint of income distribution but is incidental from a political standpoint.

I am going to pay relatively slight attention to a number of non-income-tested alternatives that are considered by many to be superior to the existing welfare system. In particular, family allowances are very popular in some other countries and received consideration in the United States during the 1950s and early 1960s. Also, the idea of a credit income tax—a reform of the income tax and welfare systems joined together—was aired by Senator McGovern during his presidential campaign. He proposed a refundable tax credit of $1,000 per person together with income tax simplification and reform.

## PROBLEMS WITH THE EXISTING WELFARE SYSTEM

In examining the problems with the existing system the chief thing to keep in mind is that in two senses there is acute disagreement about what the problems of the system are. First, characteristics of the system that some people regard as faults, others perceive as virtues. Second, there is great disagreement over the weight that ought to be attached to characteristics of the system that everybody regards as problems.

## Program Characteristics

Liberal critics contend that the main problem with the welfare system is the inadequacy of benefits, particularly in a number of states of the old Confederacy. AFDC is almost unique in that the federal government makes close to an open-ended commitment to match expenditures of the states but allows the states complete authority to determine benefit levels. Consequently, variations in benefits are enormous, with some states paying benefits five times as high as those paid in other states. The level of benefits in the low-benefit states is insufficient to keep body and soul together. Also, geographic variability results in inequities among people similarly situated and creates incentives to migration, although nobody has documented that geographic variability in benefit levels has actually caused significant migration.

In addition to geographic differences, benefits vary across demographic groups, for example, between one- and two-parent families. AFDC requires that payments be made available to single parents with dependent children, but payments are also made available to two-parent families in which one of the parents is disabled. In fact, about a quarter of the caseload in the basic AFDC program consists of two-parent families in which one parent is either disabled or otherwise unable to work. Half the states, including far more than half the total number of AFDC beneficiaries, also provide benefits to two-parent families in which neither parent is disabled or incapacitated but the father is unemployed. The eligibility restrictions, however, are quite severe, and participation among the eligible population is low; only about 150,000 such families are aided throughout the states. Thus, welfare is available to single-parent families at varying levels of benefits in different states, but not to most two-parent families with equally low incomes. (Note that the program for unemployed fathers is clearly discriminatory and unconstitutional. One policy issue is how to modify the program so that it deals equitably with families, regardless of whether the father or mother is unemployed.)

Welfare benefits also vary capriciously across income levels. This is an indirect way of alluding to the "notch problem" that exists under Medicaid and under the Unemployed Father Program in AFDC. Medicaid eligibility typically is keyed to welfare eligibility, and the benefits in many states are quite generous. If family income rises just sufficiently to make one ineligible for welfare, one loses access to all Medicaid benefits. The result is a very high tax or benefit reduction rate. In fact, the rate is mathematically infinite over a certain small range. Some states have "spend-down" provisions under which an individual who becomes ineligible because of increased income can subtract medical expenditures from that income. In such cases, the state pays for medical expenditures equal in value to the difference between income net of medical expenditures and the income eligibility level under Medicaid. Also, some states provide payments to the "medically indigent," who are defined simply as individuals with low income, even if they are not on welfare. These measures cushion the notch effect somewhat. But Medicaid still imposes what amounts to a 100 percent tax rate for Medicaid alone. The Unemployed Father Program also has a notch effect because of the rule that terminates eligibility for a beneficiary who works more than 100 hours per month. That 101st hour of work can reduce the individual's annual income by several thousand dollars.

Thus, different program characteristics entail different sorts of problems. The problem of geographic variability is distinct from problems created by variations across demographic or income groups.

Another aspect of the existing welfare system that results in inequities and perverse incentives is the lack of what is called "eligibility to the break-even." The break-even point is the income level at which a family loses eligibility for benefits. In most states the income a family must have to secure initial eligibility is much lower than the break-even point. This feature has at least two unfortunate effects. One family may be eligible for welfare while another with identical income is not.

This inequity will arise if one family previously had an income low enough to secure eligibility, but the other did not. The second unfortunate consequence is that any family with income just below the break-even point faces a serious risk if its income rises above the break-even point. In that case, it cannot regain eligibility if its income declines unless income falls all the way to the level required for initial eligibility. This provision discourages additional work, but the strength of the effect is hard to estimate.

Another characteristic that draws criticism from liberals and conservatives alike is the administrative cumbersomeness of the welfare system. AFDC is set up with only broad federal rules for administration. The states are allowed considerable discretion to establish their own administrative rules. These vary greatly from one state to another and are very complex in most states. As a result, the individual caseworker typically exercises enormous discretion in administering the program so that there is variability not only across states because of different rules but also within a state because of differing interpretations of given rules. Moreover, the fact that the program is state-administered means that there is relatively little exchange of records among states, which creates problems of error and abuse: error by administrators and abuse by recipients.

## Program Effects

One of the major issues in the welfare reform debate is the impact of the entire welfare system

on work incentives. A number of years ago I prepared a short pamphlet for Brookings called,
"Why is Welfare So Hard to Reform?" The theme
of the pamphlet was the issue of work incentives
arising in substantial part from the cumulation
across programs of benefit reduction rates. Under
an income-tested program, as income increases
benefits decline either smoothly or abruptly. If a
person is receiving benefits under two or more
such programs at the same time, benefits from
each program will decline if the person's income
rises. Thus, the implicit tax that the reduction of
each set of benefits imposes can cumulate across
several programs. There is extensive literature on
this subject. The evidence seems to indicate that
things are not quite as bad in practice as they
appear to be on paper. Nevertheless, they can be
quite bad, partly because of the smooth reduction
in benefits under cash assistance programs as
earnings rise and partly because of the abrupt loss
of benefits as eligibility is entirely lost, for example, under Medicaid.

It's interesting that there is a discordance between popular beliefs about work incentives and
the results of research on groups subject to work
incentives. People seem most concerned about the
potential impact of these programs on the supply
of males in the work force. There is less concern
with female heads of household, and there is little
concern with the aged in this respect; they are not
expected to work. However, research on the ef-

fects of welfare on labor supply indicates that the aged and female heads of household seem to be the most sensitive groups, and prime-age males seem to be the least sensitive.

Work incentives can be influenced in two ways in the short run. As the net wage associated with work declines, labor supply tends to fall. Economists call this response the substitution effect. In addition, the provision of income support raises the income of the poor, and people tend to spend part of their increased income on the consumption of more leisure, a fancy way of saying that they work less. Economists call this response the income effect. Note that the income effect poses an immediate dilemma in terms of work incentives: the more adequate the benefit, the smaller the incentive to work, all other things being equal. It would appear that lowering the benefit reduction rate—the rate at which benefits are decreased as earnings increase—should have a positive effect on work incentives, because each additional hour (or week or month) of work would yield a higher net increase in income. One of the interesting findings of the Income Maintenance, or negative income tax, Experiments is that this is true on an individual basis but not in the aggregate. In fact, in a system with low benefit reduction rates, which would appear to be most conducive to work, the total reduction in labor supply is greater than in a system with high benefit reduction rates. For any given benefit payable to fami-

lies with no other income, a low benefit reduction
rate will result in the provision of benefits to more
people than will a high benefit reduction rate.

Suppose, for example, we compare two plans,
both of which guarantee $5,000 to a family of four
with no outside income. Plan A has a benefit
reduction rate of 66 2/3 percent. Plan B has a benefit reduction rate of 40 percent. Plan A will provide some support to families whose income is
$7,500 or less. Plan B will provide some support to
families with income up to $12,500. For all fami-
lies with earnings below $7,500, Plan B has a
lower benefit reduction rate than does Plan A and
in this respect has better work incentives. Even
over this range, Plan B provides more income than
does Plan A and in this sense has weaker work incentives. On theoretical grounds one cannot be
sure which plan has stronger work incentives for
families with earnings below $7,500. For families
with income between $7,500 and $12,500—a much
more thickly populated range of the income distribution than the part below $7,500—Plan B clearly
has weaker work incentives than Plan A, which
has no direct effect at all. Plan B increases the income and reduces the net wage (through its 40 percent benefit reduction rate) of people in the $7,500
to $12,500 income range, both of which effects re-
duce work incentives. Thus, Plan B, which looks
more conducive to work than Plan A, turns out to
be less conducive to work, in fact. Now it is clear
that these are really different plans. Plan B is
more generous and this generosity manifests itself

in larger income effects which discourage work. It would be fairer to compare Plan A with a plan that transferred the same amount to beneficiaries but, like Plan B, had a benefit reduction rate of only 40 percent. Let's call this Plan C. Clearly, Plan C would have to provide less help to families with no outside income. Unfortunately, it turns out that even if Plan A and Plan C have the same transfer cost, Plan C may have greater work disincentive effects than Plan A. This finding isn't earth shaking from the standpoint of economic analysis, but it does have considerable significance in evaluating the trade-offs among different welfare reform objectives.

Another major effect of existing programs is their impact on family stability. The existing welfare system, on its face, seems to encourage family instability because benefits are more apt to be paid to single-parent than to two-parent families. A two-parent family confronted by illness or unemployment can often do better financially if the father leaves than if he stays. Until the Seattle-Denver Income Maintenance Experiments were conducted, little evidence had been available on whether family stability would increase or decrease if aid were offered uniformly and without stigma to both one- and two-parent families. The surprising finding of these experiments is that a negative income tax benefit offered without stigma on equal terms to one- and two-parent families initially seemed to increase the rate of family breakup. This apparent discrepancy be-

tween common sense and experimental results
was as dramatic as any that have been revealed
through social science research.

The initial explanation advanced for this discrepancy was that the negative income tax experiments produced an "independence effect"—an
opportunity for unhappy partners to separate
that is absent under the existing program. At
present, couples contemplating separation know
that welfare may be available but in varying
degrees are averse to the stigma attached to
claiming welfare. In contrast to the existing system, the Seattle-Denver experiments provided
payments without stigma because of the circumstances under which benefits were paid. Accord-
ingly, the negative income tax payments were
worth more than an equivalent amount of welfare.
Furthermore, they were available with certainty
under circumstances the administrators were
scrupulous in explaining, while there was always
the chance that an application for welfare might
be turned down.

While one can rationalize the results of the
negative income tax experiments, there were some
rather anomalous patterns that raise questions
about the reliability of the findings of increased
family instability, even under the special conditions of an experimental negative income tax.
There were big differences in responses not only
over time but also across ethnic groups. The increase in family instability among blacks con-
tinued for three years. Among whites the effect
stopped after the second year and reversed in the

third. And the effect for Hispanics was never statistically significant. This great variability raises the question of whether such effects are artifacts of the experiment. Let me stress, however, that the research contractor has looked for explanations for the results, but the findings seem to be robust.

I think the major issue is the unclear relationship between the negative income tax plan tested in these experiments and the kind of program that would exist in the real world. To what extent did the differences between the conditions under which the experimental payments were made and those that would obtain in *any* real-world program produce the independence effects? The experiments contained no requirement that recipients register for work or accept employment. Both are standard features of welfare as it exists today or as it would likely become under any reform plan acceptable to Congress. The experiments did not enforce child support. The effort to locate, and to obtain support from, absent fathers is an increasingly important element of the AFDC program. Its absence from the experiments is significant. In any case, the conflict remains between a common sense view of the present system and the experimental findings, which seem to call that view into question.

There are other features of the present system that must be considered if any practical reform is to be accomplished. For example, the system is federal but the programs are managed by the states. The states hire the staff and set the policy of a program that is politically very sensitive. How the poor are treated, what is required of them, and what restrictions are placed on the program all have great social and economic significance, in part because of their bearing on the labor supply of the low-income population. Furthermore, the states have a bureaucracy on their payrolls, which is a political factor of considerable importance. More than 100,000 people are involved in the administration of AFDC and the related Medicaid program.

Federal financial involvement in welfare programs also varies considerably from one state to another. To reduce cross-state variation in benefits we would have to either increase or decrease benefits, or do a little bit of both. Increasing benefits to the levels paid in the more generous states would raise transfer costs prohibitively. Also, in the states with the lowest wages and/or the lowest benefits, large increases in benefits would probably have a significant effect on labor supply. Payment of benefits in Alabama or Mississippi or South Carolina corresponding to those paid in Oregon or New York would place a substantial fraction of the labor force in the first group of states on some form of income assistance. Leveling down also creates serious problems. The more generous states have made an enormous financial commitment to income support for low-income people. This commitment rests on their political beliefs about the levels of benefits that are necessary and proper to pay people, and they simply would not stand for leveling down. Politically, if federal support were held to the levels now paid in the lower benefit states, those states that now pay high benefits could not afford to maintain payment levels purely out of their own resources. The lesson is that uniform federal support is not practical because we cannot level up, and we cannot level down. As a practical matter, a reformed welfare system must be able to accommodate substantial variation in benefits across the states—perhaps nearer to, but still very far from, uniformity.

## RECENT EXPERIENCE AND LESSONS LEARNED FROM IT

Even before he was inaugurated, President Carter committed himself to submit a comprehensive welfare reform proposal to Congress. Then he set a deadline of May 1, 1977, for the development of the proposal. In fact, the plan was transmitted in detail the following September. A special subcommittee, which was created to review the proposal, reported it out favorably, but then the plan was stalled in Congress; neither House acted on it.

In the middle of 1978 Congressman Ullman offered a compromise proposal which was less comprehensive than the administration's plan but nevertheless provided for reform of the system in a number of areas. That proposal did not succeed either.

The 1980 budget, submitted in January of 1979, announced the administration's intention to start the process again. The fate of this new effort is unlikely to be known until sometime in 1980.

The administration's comprehensive plan sought to provide a base level of cash assistance to all persons. It was complicated because of the fact that it was necessary to accommodate variation in benefit levels across states, and because the level of benefits and conditions of payment varied across demographic groups. The plan called for a base of federal support on top of which state supplemental payments (in the cost of which the federal government would share) would permit variations in payment levels. Combined with the reform of cash assistance was a proposed expansion of Public Service Employment targeted to recipients of cash assistance, notably to principal earners in two-parent families and adults in one-parent families in which the youngest child is fourteen or over. A substantial expansion of the Earned Income Tax Credit was also proposed.

The first lesson we learned is that a simple negative income tax or guaranteed income plan simply cannot be enacted, and it is probably bad social policy. To understand why, the information in Table 1 is very helpful. It shows the fraction of the estimated net cost of providing cash assistance to two-parent families that results because of reductions in labor supply. Net cost is the transfer cost under a set of hypothetical plans less the value of food stamps to which such families are now entitled. The hypothetical plans all provide a basic benefit to families with no earnings or other income of $4,200, or the amount of the basic bene-

## Table 1. Assistance Costs Before and After "Reform" and Changes in Earnings for Two-Parent Families*
### (billions of 1975 dollars)

| | Benefit Reduction Rate | | | | |
|---|---|---|---|---|---|
| | 40% | 50% | 60% | 70% | 80% |
| 1. Cash plus Food Stamps Before Reform | 4.8 | 4.8 | 4.8 | 4.8 | 4.8 |
| 2. Cash Assistance After Reform | 14.0 | 10.6 | 8.6 | 7.3 | 6.8 |
| 3. Net Increase in Cash Assistance (line 2 − line 1) | 9.2 | 5.8 | 3.8 | 2.5 | 2.0 |
| 4. Estimated Decline in Earnings Due to Reform | 3.5 | 2.5 | 1.9 | .6 | .7 |
| 5. Net Increase in Income (line 3 − line 4) | 5.7 | 3.3 | 1.9 | 1.9 | 1.3 |
| 6. Efficiency Index (line 5 divided by line 3) | 62% | 57% | 50% | 76% | 65% |

*Figures represent 100 percent participation in available programs. Numerous "out-of-computer" adjustments have not been made so that the net increase in assistance shown here does not exactly equal the net increase in assistance which we estimate this program would have caused in 1975.

The basic benefit level in each state is set equal to the maximum amount paid in AFDC in that state in 1975 plus the bonus value of food stamps, but not to be less than 65 percent of the poverty line. The state with the highest benefit levels (other than Alaska and Hawaii) paid about 100 percent of the poverty line.

Source: "The Use of Income Maintenance Experiment Findings in Public Policy, 1977–1978," in *Proceedings of the Industrial Relations Research Association 1979*, John Todd and Henry Aaron, eds.

fit provided under AFDC plus food stamps, whichever is greater. The hypothetical plans differ in their benefit reduction rates from 40 percent to 80 percent.

Now there are two ways to look at the effects of such plans on labor supply. One makes the effects look small; the other makes the effects look large. The first method reports the percentage change in work effort of households affected by the experiments. While there is some dispute about precisely who is affected (for example, are people affected whose income is just above the level at which benefits cease to be paid?), there is general agreement that the labor supply of fathers in two-parent families is reduced less than 10 percent. Most people work a little less but few stop working altogether. The stereotype of the welfare bum parked in front of a color TV, beer in hand, is inconsistent with the results of the experiments. Mothers in two-parent families reduce their employment for pay proportionately more but absolutely less than do fathers, because they work little to start with. Wives participating in the negative income tax experiments work little because in general it is not possible for a couple with two full-time earners to be eligible for cash assistance under the experiments. Viewed from this standpoint, cash assistance does not have a large effect on labor supply.

From another standpoint, the results are rather different. Table 1 shows the amount that two-parent families received in 1975 in the form of cash assistance and food stamp benefits, totaling

$4.8 billion; the amount two-parent families would have received under the hypothetical alternative plans; and the difference between these amounts. Line 4 shows the reduction in earnings attributable to each plan, estimated with the HEW cost-estimating model and using behavioral parameters calculated from the Seattle-Denver experiment. The HEW model is a sophisticated tool for simulating how people will alter their labor supply in response to changes in their income and net wages. It can be used for estimating the cost and effects on labor supply of both income maintenance and employment programs. Line 5 shows the net increase in income of the family—the increase in cash assistance less the decline in earnings. Line 6 is the "efficiency index"—the ratio of the net increase in the income of the family to the net increase in assistance to the family, that is, the ratio of line 5 to line 3.

Between a quarter and a half of the additional transfer cost goes to replace reduced earnings. Whether that fraction is considered big or small is in the eye of the beholder. I would point out that in other social programs, such as Unemployment Insurance and Social Security, either we do not much care about the labor supply effects, or we actually seek them. For example, one of the major purposes of Social Security was—and from the viewpoint of many people probably still is—to get the elderly out of the labor force in order to make room for younger people in the job pool. But that is obviously not an objective of welfare. Nevertheless, it is apparent that as much as half of the

additional expenditures for two-parent families
that are occasioned by a negative income tax are
used simply to replace reduced earnings. Note
that the most efficient plan is not the one with the
lowest tax rate, nor is the least efficient plan the
one with the highest tax rate.

Politically speaking, these results kill a large
and comprehensive negative income tax for two-
parent families; Congress will not pass it.

I tried to argue that cash assistance alone will
not work. Can jobs alone work for two-parent
families? No, they cannot. This is the second lesson of welfare reform that we have learned in the
last couple of years. The jobs-alone strategy cannot work for two reasons. First, income from a job
at the minimum wage level would be significantly
lower than existing income standards for a family
of four in a number of the high-benefit states, and
it would be far below the benefit levels for larger
families in many states. The low wage would have
to be supplemented, given my prior axiom that we
cannot drastically reduce existing benefit levels.
Thus, if the wage rate is low, jobs alone will not be
sufficient to support two-parent families. That
suggests the possibility of setting the wage rate
somewhat higher than the minimum wage—high
enough to provide adequate support for larger
families. But this solution would create another
problem. It would provide very generous support,
particularly in the low-benefit states, for small
families and would be extremely attractive to millions of private-sector job holders. The result
could be what one government economist called

the "vacuum-cleaner effect"; such a public service employment program could suck into it a large number of privately employed workers and create significant disturbances in private labor markets, tending to drive up wages. Some people support a high-wage public service employment program precisely because they would like to see wages driven up. Apart from the economic arguments against such a scheme, it would run into considerable political opposition because of the disturbances it would create and because of the cost.

If neither a cash nor an employment program can work, perhaps a combination of the two can. I would like to suggest that at least on paper the combination does work. The critical question is administrative: how do we create the jobs and place people in them?

Table 2 illustrates how a combined program of liberalized cash assistance and minimum-wage jobs can assure all two-parent families an income greater than the official poverty threshold and increase the labor supply. Plans 1 and 2 in Table 2 provide cash assistance at the same levels as shown in Table 1 and do not provide public service employment for recipients of cash assistance. Plans 3 and 4 provide the same basic cash assistance as Plans 1 and 2, but they also require the principal earner in two-parent families to accept private employment or, if none is available, a public service job paying the minimum wage. Plans 1 and 3 have benefit reduction rates of 52 percent under cash assistance. Plans 2 and 4 have benefit reduction rates of 70 percent. The prereform situ-

**Table 2. Impact of Constraining Benefit Levels and Tax Rates and Providing Public Service Employment (PSE) Jobs on Work Effort of Two-Parent Families (billions of 1975 dollars)**

| | Before Reform | | After Reform | | | Effects of Reform | | |
|---|---|---|---|---|---|---|---|---|
| Plan | (1) Cash Assistance + EITC + Food Stamps | (2) Earnings** | (3) Cash Assistance + EITC | (4) Private Earnings | (5) PSE Earnings | (6) Net Change in Assistance (3) − (1) | (7) Change in Private Earnings (4) − (2) | (8) Change in Total Earnings (4) + (5) − (2) |
| 1 | 4.92 | 93.77 | 8.07* | 92.98 | 0 | +3.25 | − .79 | − .79 |
| 2 | 4.92 | 93.77 | 7.56 | 93.29 | 0 | +2.74 | − .48 | − .48 |
| 3 | 4.92 | 93.77 | 7.44* | 92.15 | 4.48 | +2.62 | −1.62 | +2.86 |
| 4 | 4.92 | 93.77 | 6.89 | 92.37 | 4.45 | +2.07 | −1.40 | +3.05 |

*Includes state supplements.

**Includes recipients of cash, food stamps, Earned Income Tax Credit (EITC), or special PSE jobs either before or after reform, i.e., the affected population. Excluding those who received only the EITC reduces preform earnings to $22.31 billion and reduces the decrease in private earnings in Plan 4 from $1.40 billion to $.59 billion.

Source: "The Use of Income Maintenance Experiment Findings in Public Policy, 1977–1978," in *Proceedings of the Industrial Relations Research Association 1979*, John Todd and Henry Aaron, eds.

ation, shown in columns 1 and 2, by definition is the same under all of the plans. The postreform situation, shown in columns 3, 4, and 5, and the effects of reform, shown in columns 6, 7, and 8, are quite different. All of the plans reduce private earnings, but the two plans offering public service employment reduce them less than do the two plans that do not offer jobs. But total labor supply actually increases (column 8) if two-parent families are offered public service employment and required to accept it as a condition for cash assistance on an unreduced schedule.

The appeal of a plan that raises the income of two-parent families above the poverty level and increases the labor supply is obvious. The fact that these simulations indicate that it is possible to achieve both goals helps explain why virtually all welfare reform plans developed lately combine job creation and work requirements with liberalized cash assistance for two-parent families.

Another lesson we have learned is that simplicity is unachievable. The wide variation in benefits across states cannot be completely eliminated because of the cost involved and because of the political importance of retaining employment for state welfare workers. In addition, simplicity is probably undesirable in terms of the objectives we seek. We do not really want to treat the aged and mothers of young children the same way we treat two-parent families with two prime-age potential earners. In the former case we are quite willing to provide high levels of guaranteed income and have high tax rates; in the latter case we are not.

The final lesson is that welfare reform has no natural political constituency. Although the poor can play on the national conscience successfully at times, they do not organize themselves or vote to the extent that other groups do; in any event, there aren't enough of them to wield a lot of political power. Fiscal relief is important because it is the side payment necessary to create a political constituency at the state level that supports welfare reform. In fact, fiscal relief was responsible for much of the complexity of the welfare reform plan initially proposed by the Carter administration a couple of years ago.

Until early 1980 efforts were still being made to develop a compromise proposal with the following features: a federal minimum benefit level for single-parent families, universal benefits for two-person families under cash assistance, Public Service Employment for two-parent families, an expanded Earned Income Tax Credit, and provision of fiscal relief. These efforts terminated with President Carter's declaration of intent in March 1980 to balance the budget.

Several other ideas for welfare reform have not been pursued. One is a credit income tax, which goes back to Lady Rhys Williams in England and James Tobin in the United States. Irving Garfinkel, director of the University of Wisconsin Poverty Center, is now a strong supporter of the idea. The credit income tax represents an attempt to simplify the welfare and income tax systems simultaneously. This plan would establish refundable credits as a base on top of which income would be taxed proportionately. The plan put forward in 1972 by Senator McGovern during his campaign for the Democratic presidential nomination is one example of this approach, but not by any means the only way in which it could be done. Unfortunately, the virtues of the credit income tax are also its fatal flaws. Simplification results in massive redistribution relative to our present system, which is loaded with all kinds of special rules, exceptions, and treatments according to how income is earned, how it is spent, the kinds of property the individual possesses, and so on. Simplicity, while having considerable aesthetic and analytic appeal, has very little political appeal, and a credit income tax is therefore not likely to be adopted.

Family allowances, under which the government pays bonuses to all families with children, regardless of income, is quite popular in western Europe but has found few supporters in the United States. The most illustrious exceptions are Daniel Moynihan (before he was elected to the Senate) and sociologist Alvin Schorr. Others have suggested that needy two-parent families should receive assistance through an expanded Unemployment Insurance program, because intact families should not be forced to go on welfare but should be provided similar benefits through a program that does not carry the stigma that welfare does. Neither of these approaches has gotten far because the budget costs of even modest per capita amounts of assistance are very large.

Another approach, which is of greater practical importance, is enforcement of the requirement that fathers provide child support. Under former

Secretary Califano, HEW expanded the Child Support Enforcement program. Various civil liberties issues are involved, but if they can be resolved, this approach has considerable popular appeal. Most people believe that because both parents are responsible for the creation of children, both should share in their support.

Looking back on this whole process I cannot decide whether the attempt by President Carter and former HEW Secretary Califano to achieve comprehensive welfare reform was a brilliant, if inadvertent, device for forging a consensus where none had existed before, or a terrible lost opportunity. At one level, the effort to achieve comprehensive welfare reform, like the effort to achieve comprehensive tax reform, comprehensive energy legislation, and comprehensive health insurance, represented a complete misreading of the political mood of the nation and of the capacity of the Carter Administration to move controversial legislation through Congress. The Program for Better Jobs and Income was too sweeping and too costly to pass in the late 1970s.

By seeking comprehensive reform, however, President Carter and former Secretary Califano began a process that required interdepartmental debate within the administration, that involved staff and members of several congressional committees, and that led to extensive hearings and debate throughout the nation on welfare, employment, and social services. Out of that process emerged a consensus spanning most of the Democratic and Republican parties, embodied in separate legislative proposals sponsored by Congressmen Ullman and Corman and Senators Baker, Bellmon, Danforth, and Ribicoff, that welfare reform should include a federally established minimum level of benefits for one-parent families, mandatory coverage of two-parent families, a work requirement backed up by job creation, an expanded earned-income tax credit, and fiscal relief. The dream expressed in President Carter's Program for Better Jobs and Income of a single, unitary system, aiding all of the poor and simplifying administration, is gone. It was an impossible dream from the start because of the simple fact that we do not want to treat all classes of recipients alike and we cannot ignore the historical legacy of geographically diverse benefits.

We shall never know whether welfare reform could have succeeded early in the Carter Administration had the President embraced an incremental, rather than a comprehensive, approach. Although I espoused an incremental approach at the time, I now doubt whether it would have succeeded either. Critics, I think, would have attacked any increase in welfare outlays. The comprehensive and costly Program for Better Jobs and Income persuasively presented the case for certain structural features in welfare reform but left budgetary space for critics to show that some progress toward virtually all of those goals could be achieved at less than half of the cost. The unresolved question now is whether that consensus can be transformed into legislative reality in the foreseeable future.

**Question:** Is there any hope for substantial savings in administrative costs if we reform welfare?

**Aaron:** There is hope for achieving significant savings in program costs through improved administration. The most expensive part of administering the system is measuring income. The present system avoids costs by measuring income only infrequently. This results in transfer costs that are unnecessarily high, but it saves in administrative costs. Typically, people who apply for welfare are asked to predict their income for the next month and to report any large changes in income if they occur but otherwise not to come back for a stipulated period of time. In the case of certain families it may be a month; in other cases, it may be six months or longer. This arrangement results in application of rules and checking procedures at the front end but minimal subsequent contacts. However, there is considerable evidence that people are more assiduous about reporting a decline in income than they are about reporting an increase, because the former occasions an increase in benefits and the latter occasions a decrease. The solution is monthly income reporting. The administration had such a proposal in its 1980 budget to become effective in 1982, HEW is sponsoring demonstration programs in monthly income reporting, and it is included in the welfare reform proposal. Monthly reporting normally involves some simplification in procedures, but it also increases the number of contacts. Thus, monthly reporting does not reduce administrative costs at all, but it does reduce overall program costs because fewer payments are made. Program consolidation, which was the distinguishing characteristic of the administration's proposal, results in some savings, but these are again offset by the administrative costs of monthly reporting. The costs of administering a comprehensively or incrementally reformed program probably would be within 10 to 15 percent of existing administrative costs.

**Question:** Is it possible to harness the Internal Revenue Service (IRS) to do this job and pose the threat that people who lie about their income will go to jail?

**Aaron:** It is certainly possible, but I'm not sure that we would want to. The price might be very high in nondollar terms, because the rules used by the IRS differ from those that would need to be applied to welfare. The unit that files is different, the measurement period is different, and the items to be included in income are different. Consequently, IRS procedures would have to be altered dramatically if the IRS were to deal with welfare. That leaves open the question of what sanctions to impose on people who lie about their income, which is a separate issue, it seems to me. From a purely

administrative standpoint, linking welfare to the
tax system entails at least as great a risk of
damaging the tax system as the potential benefit
of making welfare administration more efficient.

**Comment:**   Another point concerning administration is the fact that tax rates for welfare
recipients are actually much lower than what
appears on the books. What is interesting is that a
lot of the early modeling was based on the tax rates
that appeared on the books as opposed to the
actual rates, which are often not more than half or
three-quarters of those on the books. And the
whole thing started off from an unwarranted
assumption about how the program was operating.

**Aaron:**   That's right.

**Comment:**   Weak administration—if you want
to put it in those terms—does have a definite effect on work incentives.

**Aaron:**   It's highly variable across the United
States. AFDC has the same benefit reduction rate
in every state: according to law, the individual
keeps the first $30 and then faces a benefit reduc-
tion rate of two-thirds of net income over and
above work-related expenses. The actual rate differs across states and across income levels from
zero to about 50 or 55 percent, depending on each
state's rules regarding work-related expenses,
complex things called "ratable reductions," and so
forth. The basic point is that the variation is huge,
and the rate is lower than that prescribed by law.

**Question:** I understand that Moynihan anticipates some leveling effects from the administration's proposal, meaning money would be taken away from New York and given to Alabama. How would that come about?

**Aaron:** It depends on what is included in the count. If fiscal relief is included, New York does very well, because the state has spent so much on welfare. Looking at it from the other side, any system that increases transfers to low-income people in states where benefits are low is not going to do as much where benefits are high, such as New York. Those benefits are going to have to be paid for by increased taxes somewhere, and some of the burden will fall on the citizens of New York. Thus, the high-benefit states probably would get a large amount of fiscal relief, but they tend to lose in terms of net fiscal flow.

**Question:** You stayed away from social services and their relation to the welfare problem. What role did social services play in recent discussions?

**Aaron:** Welfare reform has gone through a number of generations. In the early 1960s emphasis was placed on improving social services and linking them to cash assistance. Indeed, the part of Nixon's family assistance plan that didn't pass went through an interesting evolution. It was initially based on what was called the "income strategy," the belief that government should provide cash and let people spend it as they wish. The

House then changed the plan and put most of the added outlays into social services. The unique characteristic of the current debate is the linkage of jobs and cash assistance; historically, an interesting second feature of it is the fact that scant attention has been paid to social services.

**Question:** One of your last statements in summing up the lessons we have learned was that cash and jobs can work. In terms of the sorts of problems that you identified with the existing system, exactly what does "work" mean? Would a combination of cash and jobs reduce the poverty gap to zero? Would it do away with notch effects entirely? Would it do away with geographical differences and the inadequacy of benefits? How serious would these problems continue to be, and how much residual pressure would there be even if a cash-plus-jobs program were enacted? It seems to me that most of the criticisms of the existing system are left intact under this kind of plan.

**Aaron:** I think the main question is whether we can create jobs in sufficient numbers, place people in them, maintain adequate work discipline, and assure that people do not remain permanently in these jobs. The associated administrative problems are extremely serious. With the increase in targeting of jobs for the poor, under Title II of the Comprehensive Employment and Training Act (CETA), there has tended to be a big shortfall in filling available slots. I would like to know more about that because it bears directly on the problem of creating jobs for this population.

As far as the objectives of welfare reform are concerned, we can make progress in meeting each one. We can reduce geographic inequity, eliminate some notches (by means of revisions in the Unemployed Father Program), reduce discrepancies in the treatment of families of different compositions, and simplify rules. Monthly reporting is desirable, even though it costs a little more to administer, because it can improve the equity with which benefits are distributed.

Thus, I think we can make progress on all the objectives of welfare reform—with the one exception of program consolidation—by means of the incremental kind of reform now being discussed. Ten years hence critics of the welfare system will still be able to point to differences in benefits, and I'm sure other problems will have arisen with the jobs program, if it is enacted. We won't have solved them all, but at least we will have made them less serious. We probably will not be able to solve all the problems, partly because we have mutually inconsistent goals which are weighted differently by different people.

**Question:** Who would be responsible for the administration of the jobs and cash assistance program? You seem to imply that CETA will provide jobs. Is that a foregone conclusion?

**Aaron:**  People have mentioned the work incentive (WIN) agencies as a possibility.

**Question:**  What role, if any, should research play in welfare reform? Can it provide solutions to some of these problems or is this not now the area where social science research is most applicable to public policy?

**Aaron:**  I think the present obstacles are political, not informational, with the significant possible exception of the puzzling finding about family stability. I say "possible exception" because it seems to me that this issue is going to be used in a forensic manner. It will be used as an argument by people who have reached predetermined conclusions. It's a fascinating intellectual puzzle that will probably command attention for quite a while, but I don't think it will be the decisive issue.

The principal problem right now is that although most people agree on the major contents of the package, they differ in how they would weight them. Some people may want to put more money into cash assistance reform and less into jobs or vice versa. And many don't want to spend any more money on welfare than they now do, however desirable the reforms. It's not clear that Congress or the American people, who Congress represents, are willing to contemplate putting additional scarce resources into these programs. A key member of the Senate Finance Committee staff once told me that on the subject of welfare all senators are statesmen: they make their decisions free of political constraint, according to the dictates of their conscience. The fact is that there are no powerful lobbies on the issue of welfare. I think most representatives are similarly detached from political constraints. Their concerns about inflation, slow growth, balanced budgets, and so on will tend to steer them away from putting more money into the welfare sysem. I hope progress can be made. Welfare is an issue that we have been butting our heads against for ten years and if we come away from it with nothing in terms of legislative changes affecting the non-aged population, the failure will be quite depressing. We did come away with SSI in 1972, and I suppose the 1977 reform in food stamps could be considered a significant change.

**Question:** Hasn't there been a major expansion and, in this sense, a reform of welfare in recent years?

**Aaron:** There was a large increase in participation in AFDC during the late 1960s and early 1970s, and there was a big expansion in food stamps, in terms of both legislation and participation, but in neither case was there any expansion in the late 1970s. Thus, the picture depends on the frame of reference. Comparing the present system with the late 1960s, everything you say is 100 percent correct. There has been an enormous extension of coverage and an increase in the adequacy of benefits over that period. The trends for the future, I think, are different. Real expenditures on AFDC have been declining since the mid-1970s, and I think that trend will continue for the next few years. Food stamps are indexed to food prices; participation could increase, particularly since purchase requirements have been dropped, but I would not expect further increases in benefits. We are still left with very low benefits in many areas of the country. There are several serious structural anomalies in the program that can be cleaned up at a cost that is not prohibitive relative to current expenditures in this area. An increase of 10 to 15 percent in expenditures on these programs would be sufficient to make them work much better.

**Question:** It seems to me that nobody is really overjoyed with CETA or with WIN. Do you see any possibility for completely new kinds of job programs?

**Aaron:** The only approach that seems to warrant attention is provision of private sector tax credits. Last year's tax reform bill expanded the employment credit. Two or three years hence, we will begin to see a flow of analyses. If they suggest that tax credits have had a significant effect, perhaps we will go in that direction, but I don't really foresee a large new initiative with respect to public service jobs for adults.

**Question:** Is there any possibility of relating jobs to other priorities, such as mass transportation or other energy-saving investments?

**Aaron:** I don't think so. One should not underestimate the impetus for modest fiscal thinking generated by the present budgetary climate.

**Question:** If a modest expansion of programs—10 to 15 percent—would roughly solve the problem, does that imply that poverty in the United States has essentially been eliminated?

**Aaron:** No, it doesn't. It implies a judgment that income equalization is not the agenda of welfare reform. Welfare reform is aimed at providing assistance at a chosen aggregate level so that bad incentives are avoided and the program can be administered equitably and reasonably. I think we can make significant advances on these fronts at modest costs. A program designed to raise the income level of low-income people significantly would obviously be expensive, but I think that is a different agenda from welfare reform. It is essential to separate these agendas if welfare reform is to stand a chance of enactment.

# 3

## *National Health Insurance*

AT THE START OF HIS ADMINISTRATION, PRESIDENT
Carter committed himself to sweeping reforms in
three areas: taxes, welfare, and health. To this for-
midable list he shortly added energy. Tax reform
has not been a conspicuous success; Congress cut
taxes but did little reforming, unless undoing
some of the reforms of the late 1960s and early
1970s is itself regarded as reform. The comprehensive plan to reform welfare did not pass even one
house of Congress, and it was supplanted by an incremental but ambitious plan whose fate at this
time is still in doubt. After internal discussion of a
health plan that would have cost over $30 billion,
the administration advocated one that would cost
roughly $20 billion, far less than the cost of Sena-
tor Kennedy's more extensive plan, but still
probably too rich for Congress's post-Proposi-
tion-13 taste.

During the course of his campaign, President Carter promised to bring out a national health insurance plan. I think one has to ask why he made this commitment and why there has been so little progress in resolving this important issue over the thirty years that it has been on the national political stage. The promise of a national health insurance plan was an important element in cementing labor support during the campaign, and one should not underestimate the role of labor and Democratic party politics in the current discussions. More broadly, national health insurance is the last outstanding issue on the New Deal agenda. The goal of the item as it appears on that agenda is to provide all Americans with financial access to medical care. Approximately 25 million Americans have no health insurance coverage; that many or more have inadequate coverage (depending on one's definition of inadequate) in terms of the range of services covered by their plans. That is the motivating force within the Democratic party. Another reason why national health insurance is a prominent issue right now transcends political boundaries; it is the sense that the health industry in general is very poorly organized and suffused with perverse incentives, and that, as a result, much of the health care that people receive is inappropriate or inefficiently provided. In this context, national health insurance is regarded as the key to reorganization of a major industry with a total budget that is approaching $200 billion.

The source of much of the inefficiency in the health industry can be traced to third-party reimbursement, which frees all key decision makers in the industry from the need to consider cost in deciding what services to provide. This is especially true with respect to hospital care; it is less true with respect to outpatient physician services. Over 90 percent of hospital services are now reimbursed by third-party payers: either private insurers or government (federal, state, or local). Another element is the sense that the proliferation of specialists and the relative paucity of primary-care physicians lead to more costly and less effective service than would otherwise be possible. Furthermore, the requirement that services be provided by physicians when in fact they could be provided by less highly trained personnel means that people living in areas where physicians, for one reason or another, have been reluctant to locate have reduced access to health care.

The high cost of a national health insurance plan explains, at least in part, why it has languished in Congress. Recently, the fear that costs are out of control has been a major force behind the revival of interest in a national health plan. The budgetary cost is high because major expenditures that are now handled in private budgets would tend to be moved to the public budget. Precisely how much should be moved is an important aspect of the debate. National health insurance would also be expensive in terms of the additional real resources that would be absorbed by the health sector; the resource cost is a great deal smaller than the budgetary cost. It is the budgetary cost that gives people the most pause for two reasons. People are concerned about the absolute size of the public sector and the rates of taxation they must bear. Furthermore, economists have not succeeded in persuading people that they should think more about real resource costs. Although former HEW Secretary Califano, President Carter, and the White House staff have all ached to argue that the real resource cost of a national health insurance plan would be small and possibly even negative in the long run, analysts have persuaded them that such an argument would not be defensible at this time. Nevertheless, real resource costs would be a great deal smaller than they appear to be. A national health insurance plan might change the way services are provided. It would also regulate reimbursement, but in the first instance such controls would not affect resource costs; they could reduce budget costs over the long run by reducing excess payments (rents, in economic jargon) that physicians now receive and by reducing the frequency with which procedures that promise few benefits are prescribed.

A national health insurance package only for the poor, providing them with free care, is calculated to cost approximately $15 billion a year. An alternative plan would provide catastrophic coverage, that is, full coverage for medical expenses over a certain large amount, for example, $1,500 a year. This type of plan would cost about $8 billion a year. Various other items could be added to the package to make a more comprehensive plan. Providing noncatastrophic benefits for individuals above the poverty level pushes the cost up into the range of the administration's original plan —$30 to $35 billion a year in 1980 dollars. This figure represents additional budget expenditures; real resource expenditures are much smaller. If we want to avoid cost sharing (where patients pay part of the cost of health care out-of-pocket when they receive it), the costs increase in leaps and bounds. Organized labor seems to have a fixed commitment to avoid cost sharing; the result of having no cost sharing would be dramatically higher budget costs and significantly higher real resource costs.

The controversy over national health insurance involves six major issues, which reflect the primary concerns in health policy today. The importance and complexity of these issues are part of the reason that comprehensive national health insurance will probably not be introduced in the foreseeable future. Given the rather short supply of willingness to make political leaps of faith at the present time, the demands of national health insurance are just too great. In addition, a large-scale national health plan would require the resolution of a host of complex issues on which powerful interests have entrenched and opposing views.

The six areas of controversy are (1) benefits and cost sharing, (2) system reform, (3) the state role, (4) administration, (5) reimbursement, and (6) financing. These issues overlap. Also, with all of them cost is a dominant concern because health is expensive and tax resources, scarce in the most bullish of times, are very limited these days.

## BENEFITS AND COST SHARING

With respect to benefits, there is general agreement that any national health plan that merits the name has to cover all inpatient hospital services, except cosmetic surgery. To avoid perverse incentives (specifically, incentives to perform any medical services in the hospital), it is also necessary to provide coverage of outpatient services for acute medical problems.

### Benefits

Several questions arise with respect to specific benefit areas. One of these is preventive services, such as routine physicals and counseling, family planning, and maternal and child or well-baby care. Recent studies examining the cost-effectiveness of preventive health services conclude that the value of preventive services is much smaller than previously thought; the Institute of Medicine has drastically reduced the frequency of recommended routine screening and checkups. The additional cost of including a broad range of preventive services in a health insurance plan can run as high as $11 billion a year. In any event, there is a good deal of difficulty in distinguishing preventive services from others: if an individual has visited a physician, who is to know whether the physician performed a routine checkup or examined an allegedly acute problem?

Several types of nonmedical preventive health services involving the environment, occupational safety and health, and personal habits are thought to have an important bearing on health, although there is not a great deal of strong evidence to this effect. Unfortunately, the costs of attempting to change people's habits are high—and indeed the technology for doing so effectively is hard to come by at the present time. In any event, even a fairly generous national health insurance plan would be likely to include a restrictive package of preventive health services.

A second benefit area includes mental health and alcohol and drug abuse services. At present, most health insurance plans do not cover these services very well. They are expensive, and if the current financial barriers were removed, the demand for them might be quite large. If these services are covered, what should be the maximum amount of services that people can receive in a given year, and what should be the mix between inpatient and outpatient care? It is estimated that the cost of providing a full package of mental health and drug and alcohol abuse coverage under national health insurance could run well over $10 billion a year. Note that these costs are in addition to the basic costs of over $15 billion for a good package of services for the poor, $8 to $10 billion for catastrophic coverage, and additional funds for noncatastrophic benefits for those who are not poor.

A third benefit area of some uncertainty is outpatient prescription drugs. This is an important area in view of the fact that current health care has been criticized for inducing admissions to hospitals simply because inpatient drugs are covered and outpatient drugs are not well covered. Many drug therapies are very costly, and physicians may admit their patients to hospitals so that they can secure third-party reimbursement. Again, the question of coverage is "how many and on what terms?" There is a range of possibilities, from no coverage, to coverage of selected drugs, to full coverage. As for the terms of coverage, the possibilities include a deductible, copayment, or no cost sharing. The costs are large. If only a few drugs that are widely prescribed and particularly costly are covered and a deductible is required, the cost is about $3 billion a year; without a deductible the cost goes up to $8 billion a year. If all drugs are covered, the cost goes up to $13 billion a year.

A benefit area that is even more uncertain is dental care. The plans I have discussed so far do not cover dental services except for surgical procedures performed in a hospital. But there is a widespread belief that bad teeth are a cause of bad health and that it would be desirable to cover less serious dental procedures as well as surgical ones. The problem here is that there is an enormous backlog of unmet dental needs. The reason, in part, is that dental services are highly price-elastic, according to the preliminary findings of the Rand Health Insurance Experiment. Consequently, lowering the price of dental services could release this backlog. Estimates of costs are so high that almost everybody agrees that under a comprehensive health plan dental care should be offered, if at all, only through certain sources, such as schools or clinics, serving particular target groups.

I will mention only in passing another benefit area (which is now covered only partially), and that is rehabilitation. It includes nursing homes, which serve a very large population of individuals who are unlikely to recover their health and for whom the capacity to absorb services is almost infinite. I think it is widely felt that rehabilitation is, again, an elastic service that is both important and very difficult to define for purposes of a health plan.

I have thus far not discussed long-term care, because it is not a purely medical concern. Instead, it is a complex mixture of social services, medical care, and counseling; moreover, care of the aged is certain to growth both in urgency and cost as the number of aged increases. It will have to be dealt with through some device other than health insurance or a health-financing plan.

## Cost Sharing

The most divisive issue concerning benefits is cost sharing. There are two perspectives from which cost sharing is seen as desirable: the economist's and the politician's. The economist wants to retain price consciousness in the demand for health care, at least for those above the lowest income level, in order to curtail the demand for services that produce meager benefits. The politician wants to keep costs off the budget. The political perspective is much more salient in terms of government planning, whereas from an analytical standpoint the economic perspective may be of more interest.

There are at least three types of cost sharing. Deductibles require that people pay all of the initial costs of certain kinds of health services. Coinsurance requires that they pay a fixed percentage of total cost. Copayments require that they pay a fixed dollar amount per unit of service purchased. In a certain sense, cost sharing is the defining issue for the benefit structure. If cost sharing is large, the resulting plan, by definition, provides catastrophic coverage; minimal cost sharing marks a universal comprehensive plan. There is some preliminary evidence that the price-rationing effect of cost sharing is much sharper in lower income brackets than it is in higher income brackets and that, therefore, cost sharing in itself is regressive in its impact on the consumption of health care. The question is what to do about that. There are at least three approaches. One is to accept those consequences. A second is to require lower cost sharing in lower income brackets. And a third—which organized labor has urged for years—is to eliminate cost sharing entirely.

## SYSTEM REFORM

At present health care is provided in myriad ways: by individual practitioners who bill on a fee-for-service basis; by groups of physicians who work together using a variety of financing devices, some of which approach prepaid plans; by full-scale health maintenance organizations (HMOs); by outpatient clinics in urban hospitals (a major source of health care for the poor); and by a number of government-sponsored programs (such as neighborhood health centers and community mental health centers). Among these modes of delivery, fees, quality of care, and the real cost of care differ a great deal.

Different fees are often charged for the same services provided by doctors in different places or by various providers in the same place. Urban doctors are paid more than rural doctors, and specialists are paid more than general practitioners—for the same services. This variation creates incentives that influence physicians' choice of location and medical specialty. The question is whether the existing distribution of physicians by geographic location and specialty is the correct one. If it is not, how should it be changed? The consensus seems to be that the existing distribution is optimal on neither score: a greater geographic dispersion of physicians would be desirable, as well as less concentration among specialties, notably surgery. Any attempt to make these changes requires consideration of how physicians are reimbursed for their services and how they choose a specialty. In the latter case, the key is choice of residency in medical school: is it desirable to attempt to change these specialties by altering the incentives for medical schools and medical school students?

One attempt to correct the geographic imbalance of physicians is the burgeoning National Health Service Corps. The program provides scholarships for medical school students on condition that, upon completion of medical school, recipients join the National Health Service Corps and serve in a medically underserved area for a stipulated period of time. The corps and the number of scholarships have expanded rapidly recently. A number of questions remains. To what extent should a device like this be used to achieve greater dispersion of physicians in the future? How long do NHSC physicians stay in underserved areas? What is the real cost of achieving dispersion?

Neighborhood health clinics and community mental health centers were introduced in the late 1960s under the Office of Economic Opportunity. The critical question in terms of national health insurance is the degree to which health care should continue to be provided through such organizations under a national health plan. Some argue that with national health insurance providing financial access to care, it would be both possible and desirable to phase out these special providers and rely on individual physicians, hospitals, and group health plans. The opposing view is that health care services simply will not be provided in certain areas (such as remote rural locations and inner-city neighborhoods) without such programs. Whereas we can muddle along or make marginal changes within existing health policy, each of these issues must be confronted directly in order to introduce a comprehensive national health plan. The administration and Congress have to take a specific stand on each, which means that they have to be willing to pay the political costs of dealing with them.

The final area that is important with respect to the general structure of the health care industry is the role that HMOs are going to play. First hailed about six or seven years ago as a panacea, then virtually stifled with delays and red tape by the federally enacted HMO program, HMOs are now beginning to expand again and are receiving some genuine encouragement from HEW through grants, loans, and support for expansion or development. Again, a national health plan would have to resolve the HMO issue— whether to continue to encourage them and, if so, how. I will discuss this issue further in regard to the issue of reimbursement.

## THE STATE ROLE

In terms of modifying existing health policy— making small modifications in Medicare, Medicaid, and other programs—the role of the states is not a major issue. However, within the context of a comprehensive health plan it moves to center stage. Furthermore, it is extraordinarily difficult to resolve because the states now play important and diverse roles in the financing of health care. All states but one have a Medicaid program; the exception is Arizona, which does not want to bear the cost of providing health care for all low-income Indians living in the state.

The total state expenditure on Medicaid for acute services is over $7 billion a year. The rest of the state Medicaid expenditure goes for long-term care and related services. The states are required to provide a certain package of benefits for acute services and are permitted to provide additional services on an optional basis. States also differ with respect to the proportion of the Medicaid program that the federal government pays. Furthermore, they can distribute their Medicaid expenditures as they choose between acute and long-term care so long as they provide the mandated basic services. As a rough generalization, states that provide minimal AFDC benefits also provide minimal acute care benefits and generous long-term care benefits. Southern states have relatively generous long-term care, spending in some cases as much as 80 percent of their Medicaid dollars on it. The Northern industrial states tend to provide generous acute care benefits for the non-aged. In analogous fashion the Southern states provide low AFDC benefits compared to those offered in the North, and before the federal government took over most of the cost of welfare for the aged, blind, and disabled, the Southern states provided relatively generous benefits for these groups.

The states also play an important regulatory role with respect to the health sector. They have traditionally licensed insurance companies, health facilities, and physicians. Recently, several states have entered the rate-setting business. If the administration's 1979 hospital cost containment bill had passed, probably many more states would have set rates, because hospitals subject to state rate setting could avoid federal regulation under that proposal. The main issue is the $7 billion now spent by states for acute care services under Medicaid. That money would be yet another addition to on-budget costs if the federal government picked it up directly. It would mean $7 billion in fiscal relief to state and local governments at a time when their finances appear to be somewhat less pinched than those of the federal government, although recession may change the picture rapidly, particularly in states that have put themselves in a financial straight jacket with self-imposed tax limitations. For that reason, it is desirable to try and move most of the $7 billion now spent by states under Medicaid. To the best of my knowledge, nobody has come up with a satisfactory way of making this transfer which does not involve undercutting the uniformity principles which have been a major force behind the national health insurance movement.

## ADMINISTRATION

Administration is an issue that analysts like to ignore, but it must be considered. Again, if one is talking about noncomprehensive, incremental modifications in the present system of health coverage in the United States, many of these questions can be finessed; at least, they are less prominent. If one is talking about a fully national plan, in which all health insurance bills go to a health agency, some of these questions do not arise. Right now everybody is talking about a plan involving continuation of employer-based plans together with umbrella coverage for those people not covered by employer plans. The administrative problems connected with this kind of plan are particularly difficult. Administration would be difficult enough in the case of the all-national plan, but it would be even more problematic for the type of plan now under consideration.

With copayments, cost sharing, or premiums that people pay for coverage under the public portion of this plan, who collects the money? There are at least two alternatives. One is the Internal Revenue Service. The other is a newly created health agency.

Another administrative issue to be addressed is the definition of the insurable unit. In a national health insurance plan this decision has an important bearing on cost if there are income-tested elements in the plan (that is, if the poor are given more generous benefits than others). In general, the smaller the unit covered, the more expensive the plan. If the unit is defined as only the nuclear family household, the plan will be more expensive than if the unit is defined to include anybody living in the household.

A third administrative consideration is the accounting period: over what period of time should income be measured for purposes of calculating whether a person has a low or high income? If the IRS is used as the administrative agency, the period will probably have to be the tax year. Whether this period is the appropriate one to use for a national insurance plan remains to be seen.

A cost-sharing plan must include provision for collecting bad debts. Again, with the IRS the usual Treasury Department or tax collection mechanism would be used. If instead a separate agency is used, what authority will it have to enforce payment?

Will premiums be collected through the withholding system? This would be desirable at least to the extent that it would be less costly administratively than setting up a new collection mechanism. However, using the tax system might expose it to the risks, unpopularity, and unique kinds of administrative problems that a national health insurance plan would generate and reduce its effectiveness in its primary role, that of tax collector.

Let me switch gears now from the public to the private part of the plan by considering the premiums that could be charged for private insurance. The cost of health insurance currently differs widely according to geographic area, demographic group, and occupational category. The question is whether to permit private insurers to provide coverage based on the particular experience of individual groups or require them to charge the same amount for health coverage in a community. Expe-

rience rating allows the private insurer to tailor
billing to the cost of each particular plan, resulting
in very high costs of coverage for small groups and
individuals. At whatever level the premium might
be set for the public plan, permitting insurance
companies to experience rate would, in effect,
allow them to cream off the good business, leaving
the expensive risks for the public sector. The result
would be the appearance, but not necessarily the
reality, that private companies can provide health
coverage more "efficiently" (really more cheaply,
because coverage is limited to less expensive risks)
than can the federal plan.

With the mixed public and private approach,
another administrative question that has pro-
found policy significance concerns rate setting
under the public plan. Employers would have to
choose between purchasing private or public coverage for their employees. The issue would then
arise as to how much employers should be charged
for public coverage. If the rate is very high, employers will choose private health insurance coverage. If the rate is low, employers will purchase
public coverage. In other words, the relative size of
employer-based private insurance coverage versus
public plan coverage is largely determined by the
level of rates for public coverage. How should the
rates be set? Should we account for the fact that
there is substantial geographic variation in the
costs of health care? How do we limit the almost in-
evitable losses that the public health plan will suf-
fer? Whatever the rates, there will always be a few
people who are very expensive to cover. Private in-

surers, even if they are required to charge the same price, will try to sell to people for whom costs are lower than the public premium rate. The higher cost people—the aged, the poor, and small groups and individuals—will require public coverage, resulting in a loss under the public plan. Should the loss be covered by a direct tax subsidy or by tax imposed on private insurance? Again, this is an administrative issue, but it bears on the structure of the whole program.

I'm going to ignore the issue of what to do about all the other health providers that are so important today: military hospitals, Defense Department coverage for civilian dependents, Veterans Administration hospitals, public health service hospitals, the Indian Health Service, and the Federal Employees Health Benefit Plan.

## REIMBURSEMENT

Reimbursement is perhaps the most difficult problem in devising a comprehensive plan. At present, a complex set of rules governs the reimbursement of physicians under Medicare and Medicaid. Rules now permit physicians to decide whether they will accept reimbursement through the public plan or bill patients directly. They may vary this decision patient-by-patient and, in effect, service-by-service. Under private insurance, reimbursement for services is generally made in fixed amounts, which are adjusted periodically. The critical question here is whether and, more particularly, how to tighten reimbursement rules in order to limit the rate at which physician billings increase. Should there be a fixed schedule of fees for particular kinds of services performed by particular kinds of doctors? If so, how should the range of fees be determined? As a condition for receiving reimbursement from the plan, should doctors be required to accept fixed fees as full payment for services, or should they be permitted to bill patients separately? If permitted to bill patients individually, should they be required to do so for all patients that they treat; in other words, should they be required to accept the fixed-fee schedule as a condition for receiving reimbursement? Should they be permitted to bill patients individually for all services or to accept reimbursement from the public plan in full? Should they be permitted to bill individually only for particular services?

Probably no arrangement would provoke greater resistance from physicians than a fixed-fee schedule and a requirement that doctors accept full reimbursement according to such a schedule. Yet any alternative would permit physicians to choose and, in effect, use the public health insurance plan as a device for covering patients unable to pay, while continuing to charge higher rates to patients able and willing to pay additional sums.

A subsidiary question is how to reimburse services provided by physicians who are employed by hospitals rather than working for themselves. At present, some physicians operating through hospitals are earning enormous incomes.

Another issue is how to reimburse acute care hospitals. The current federal system is retrospective and cost-based; that is, payment is made for costs actually incurred in the past. Any cost that is incurred in the past will tend to be reimbursed for in the future. The regulatory checks are few and weak. The basic issue here is how to limit costs when we will not let the market do the rationing. At present, over 90 percent of inpatient hospital costs are covered by third-party payers. Obviously, people are unwilling to let prices ration acute care services to any significant degree. That means that we are, in effect, preventing the market from operating. There are several possibilities for replacing the market.

Senator Kennedy and organized labor for years have advocated the establishment of fixed health care budgets for particular geographic areas. Within each area, local or areawide decision makers would determine the allocation of health care budgets among physicians and among hospitals. The problems of implementing such a budgeting technique are serious, starting with how to define geographic areas. Also, the local allocation decisions would require collection of data that are not now available.

A less comprehensive possibility is some form of cost limitation or prior budget with adjustments for utilization on a hospital-by-hospital basis. The hospital cost containment proposals that the Carter administration has been presenting over the past three years fall in this category.

One problem with them is the difficulty of adjusting for utilization. There is a substantial difference between the marginal and average costs of providing health care, and neither marginal nor average cost is uniform among hospitals. Consequently, any adjustment mechanism is heavily dependent on estimates that would be hard to make and on rules that would be hard to administer. Furthermore, adjustments for marginal cost that are set too high create incentives to circumvent the cost limit. Indeed, this is one argument being made against the administration's hospital cost containment proposal.

Additional questions concerning hospital reimbursement are how to reimburse for the costs of teaching and how to handle new investments that involve costs apart from the ongoing costs of providing acute care.

I mentioned before that a difficult question under any comprehensive plan is how to deal with health maintenance organizations. HMOs reimburse on a capitation basis; that is, in return for payment of a flat sum, the HMO provides a stipulated set of services as needed, with need being determined jointly by the HMO physicians and patients. This scheme of reimbursement does not fit in with most health insurance plans. We would have to determine how the capitation rate would be set for an HMO if we were going to use this particular form of reimbursement. There are alternatives. HMOs could be reimbursed as other health care providers are on a fee-for-service basis. However, this method would undermine one of the cost advantages of HMOs—the fact that they do not need to maintain the costly and complex records required for fee-for-service reimbursement.

## FINANCING

The financing problems of an all-federal plan, one in which all health bills are paid by a federal agency, are politically difficult, but they are not technically difficult. Any of various financing instruments can be used, such as a federal payroll tax or a premium payable to the federal administrative agency. However, technical problems do arise in connection with financing a mixed plan in which employer-based health insurance provides some coverage and a federal plan provides other coverage. It is difficult to imagine financing employer-based health insurance through any means other than premiums. The use of tax revenues would result in substantial cross-subsidies among firms.

If employers are required to provide coverage, and premiums are used as the financing mechanism, who will employers pay premiums for? Full-time workers can be members of families with one or two earners, or even more if one counts children and part-time workers. This issue has an important bearing on incentives for hiring second workers from families and part-time workers. A fixed dollar amount could be collected on behalf of every employee, but that would discourage part-time employment, because a fixed amount is a

larger marginal increment to a part-time wage
than to a full-time wage. The same amount could
be collected from both members of a working couple, but then the two-earner family would pay
twice as much as the one-earner family for health
insurance coverage. Premiums could be differen-
tiated according to family circumstances, or they
could be collected only on behalf of employees who
work more than a certain number of hours per
week. But each of these options entails administrative problems and somewhat different incentives. These are only a few of the numerous complex issues that have an important bearing on the
relative attractiveness of hiring different kinds of
workers. Also, if one accepts the usual economic
argument that the cost of health insurance will
eventually be incorporated into the overall wage
structure, then resolution of these matters will
have an impact on the take-home pay of different
classes of workers.

An issue that economists would argue is of
short- rather than long-term significance is the
proportion of the premium to be paid by employers and employees. If employers pay a large
part of the premium for a comprehensive health
plan, large firms will not be greatly affected because the mandated cost will not be significantly
different from the costs these companies now incur for health insurance. In the case of small
firms, or firms with meager insurance packages,
the mandated cost would represent a major increase in labor costs, at least in the short run.

Again, incidence theory suggests that over the longer run wage rates would be adjusted to take account of insurance costs, which raises the question of whether employers should be required to bear these costs. Yet if employees pay the costs directly, the large firms with generous plans will enjoy temporary windfalls.

A host of other financing issues must be resolved. For example, how will financing cover costs for the aged, who are very expensive to insure? What should be done about the tax code, which at present provides generous treatment of health expenses for both employers and employees? Also, what changes in the tax code should be made, if any, to discourage people from purchasing private insurance as a means of avoiding any cost sharing imposed by a national health plan? Many other questions must be addressed before any comprehensive health plan can be enacted. But I hope that the list I have run though indicates the controversial issues dividing powerful interest groups that must first be resolved.

**Question:** The assumption is usually made that all the hospitals are going to participate in national health insurance, and that leads to the problem of how to set rates. Could we consider the possibility of holding regional auctions each year in areas where there is a reasonably large number of hospitals? The hospitals would assume the risk of making acceptable bids on participating in na-

tional health insurance. High bidders would lose
the opportunity for that year to obtain some sort
of service contract.

**Aaron:**  I haven't considered that approach,
but let's do it now. It is attractive in terms of economic efficiency. However, some hospitals would
lose in that competition. What would happen to
them over the next year? If most inpatient care
could be provided by the winners, one would, in effect, be driving the losers out of business. But I
doubt that it is politically feasible to drive large
numbers of hospitals out of business. Too many
people, from holders of the high-bidding hospital's
bonds to the workers employed by the hospital,
would lose out to permit this approach to be used.

**Comment:**  I'm assuming that however we
implement this thing some sort of private sector
will exist, at least for a while. Or we could allow
losing hospitals to stay in the market but at an
additional cost to themselves or to their patients.

**Aaron:**  If the system really works and we
weed out some hospitals, I don't think that would
be politically acceptable.

**Comment:**  Patients aren't patients of hospitals; they are patients of doctors. An individual is
admitted to a particular hospital by virtue of being a patient of a certain doctor who's on the staff
of that hospital.

**Aaron:** Hospitals are employers and they're located somewhere; the constituency is going to include the particular municipality or county and the people who work in the hospital. Thus, it seems to me the political drawbacks of that approach are going to outweigh any efficiency gains.

**Comment:** But there's a potential political benefit. The strongest opposition to national health insurance is the hospitals' complaint that they're being regulated to death. We may find that the hospitals are willing to regulate each other by allowing a few of their number to die.

**Aaron:** It would be nice to be able to test that in the laboratory before unleashing it on the public.

**Comment:** It's called competition.

**Question:** You've gone through all these problems with a comprehensive plan. Why haven't you discussed some of the other plans, for example, the plans that Kennedy and Califano each support? Which of the problems you've noted apply to these other plans?

**Aaron:** I think all of these problems exist for health care policies, almost without exception. Any comprehensive health plan must deal with all of them.

**Comment:** People are trying to find the coalition that will pass some sort of bill. Much of the Carter plan borrows from other plans—a little bit from the American Medical Association plan, a little bit from the Nixon plan, a little bit from the Long bill, a little bit from the Kennedy plan, and so forth. The problem over the past five years is not that people don't want national health insurance—it's clear that they want something. The problem is finding the coalition, and these other plans reflect efforts to find such a coalition. The employer-based plan, the old Nixon plan—they're versions of the old comprehensive development insurance plan, which really was many different plans all wrapped into one on the employer's side with the various categories you mentioned. That's what's happened to the other plans too. A few years ago they came within a whisker of getting some sort of compromise bill on the floor. It fell apart at the last minute and Nixon withdrew his support. But they did come close. What they're concerned about is trying to keep people interested in it while they solve some of these cost containment problems, and so forth.

**Aaron:** I think that's exactly right, but I'm more pessimistic about the prospects. My feeling is that many people in the administration would like nothing better than if people's memories of Carter's campaign promises on the subject of national health insurance could be erased. The administration would have preferred not to intro-

duce any plan in the present budgetary atmos-
phere. But expectations have been created, starting with President Carter's campaign commitments and continuing with his commitments to
Senator Kennedy, to organized labor, to the American people: these statements made it impossible
not to send up a plan in 1979. The issue is really
what to offer considering that inflation is rising,
and Proposition 13 was passed. The President is
supporting something that will cost tens of billions of dollars for full-scale implementation.
What I think we're seeing is the retrenchment of
that commitment to the extent that is politically
feasible. The prospects of enacting any plans before 1980 were negligible. What the prospects are
after 1980 will depend on a host of events that we
cannot predict. But the current Congress seems
unwilling to commit itself even to a plan as costly
as the one introduced by President Carter.

**Comment:**   You might take a moment to indicate the difficulties of getting agreement within
the House or within the Senate on who has jurisdiction over health insurance.

**Aaron:**   There has been a long-standing ri-
valry between Senator Kennedy and Senator Tal-
madge, operating through two different committees, as to who should control health policy in the
Senate. In the House at least two committees
have jurisdiction over health policy. Moreover, all
of the plans are structured so that inevitably they

will funnel off into at least these four committees
and possibly others. Medicare and Medicaid jurisdiction is splintered in the House and certainly
any plan would affect both programs.

**Question:**   I don't understand the numbers.
The sum of all the generous cost estimates for the
possible components comes to about $150 billion;
other estimates are about $200 billion. Is the $50
billion difference attributable to the private out-
of-pocket costs, and is it distributed across all
those components?

**Aaron:**   I have not been presenting numbers
in a consistent way. The estimated total cost of
health care in 1980 is about $180 billion. The fig-
ures that I used for the various benefit increments
do not necessarily refer to current expenditures;
they are estimates of what expenditures would be
if they were included in a health insurance plan.
There is no reason why they should add up to as
little as $180 billion because they would grow; nor
is there any reason why they should add up to as
much as that because I left out whole categories of
expenditures.

**Question:**   I think $10 billion is an enormous
underestimate of expenditures relating to mental
health, alcoholism, and drug abuse. My personal
estimates range between $20 and $50 billion for
this category of health care.

You've presented a picture of enormous complexity. Given this complexity and the very high cost in lives and suffering, the politics of mistakes, and all the economic and political constraints, what sort of policy research priorities would you recommend? Obviously, we can't concentrate effectively on all these issues simultaneously. Right now we're concentrating on hospital cost containment, and that may be popular, but I'm not sure it should be the main focus of research. Do you have some views on that?

**Aaron:** We really haven't conducted much research on hospital cost containment; some work has begun on the effects of state regulations, but the national plan hasn't yet come into being. We regulate the health sector in many diverse ways, from medical education to insurance companies and licensing of health facilities. I have not seen any effort to wade through these regulations, determine how they relate to one another, and make some appraisal of their relative costs and benefits. Given the slim prospects of major institutional change or major financing change in the near future, it seems to me that one of the most useful things we could do would be to improve our understanding of how we regulate the health sector. We should look at the impacts of rate setting, not just on actual billings, but also on the provision of services and on technology in the health sector. We might be able to learn something from other countries, some of which instituted centralized budgeting procedures long ago. We could examine how the health sector has responded in these limits in other countries and what gets sacrificed at the margin.

**Question:** Is anybody doing serious research on the design of an ideal set of health care services? We've addressed the question of good and bad investments in education, particularly in higher education. Is any attempt being made to determine the return on investment for different components of health care services? Isn't a fundamental issue the confusion between rational and irrational demand for services, and can't that be resolved only by determining the relative health productivity of different kinds of care?

**Aaron:** Physicians and other health scientists are continually doing research on medical procedures, particularly new ones, in order to measure their effectiveness. There are two new centers of health technology: one is congressionally established and the other is being established within HEW. Each will try to appraise new health technologies. I don't know of any systematic attempt at present to look across existing and new technologies other than the case-by-case medical research—for example, on what coronary bypass surgery will do for subsequent health status.

Let me switch to the issue of risk analysis in environmental studies. A *National Journal* article recounts the desire of some analysts to calculate the value of human life implicit in various regulatory decisions; they are concerned about some regulations that require expenditures of tens of millions of dollars to save a single life. This mode of thinking is apparently regarded as mechanistic and cruel in many quarters. Precisely that attitude—that such modes of thinking are inhuman—leads to the belief that a person who is sick should have the best care, presumably meaning the care that, in an engineering sense, produces any marginal benefit. Most would agree that the services should be produced as efficiently as possible; if it has zero benefit, it should not be provided. But the term "benefit" is very loosely defined as anything that helps even a little.

The current health care system, from an incentive standpoint, is perfectly designed to ensure that every service that is even marginally beneficial is provided, and there is no incentive for production efficiency. There is a tension between the people who are willing to do risk-benefit analysis and those whose point of view led to the creation of a third-party reimbursement system. There are certain logical consequences of the incentives we've created and we ought not to be surprised about them or about their macro implications. What's happening now is that a debate is commencing about the structure of those incentives, and thus far I don't think we've really come to grips with it. Hospital cost containment is a piecemeal solution; it is at best an imperfect, temporary device for dealing with cost problems which the administration regards as intolerable. Thus far, we haven't really come to grips with the basic issue, which is that we're not willing to use the market or price consciousness in the health sector. This forces us to impose regulatory solutions, with all the pitfalls that they've entailed in other sectors. It's a dilemma in the true sense of the word; we don't know how to resolve it at present. I really think that the best possible outcome would be for Congress to keep on considering, but never quite to enact, cost containment. The threat might help sustain the voluntary effort of hospitals to limit hospital costs, an effort which seems so far to have held down costs somewhat. That way we could avoid the pitfalls of a questionable regulatory apparatus but still have some limitation of costs. But this is the stuff of dreams.

**Question:** Don't you think that one of the reasons the administration is so concerned about finding a short-run solution is that escalating medical costs means less money for new programs in other areas? I'm sure that President Carter, even though he may have natural proclivities in that direction, doesn't like coming out with a very conservative budget. It's not good politics to go into an election with budgets that deprive powerful groups of things they want.

**Aaron:** I agree with you. The hospital cost containment plan is the result of a sense that something must be done to hold down hospital costs and an awareness that structural reforms, if they work at all, will take many years to be effective. Increases in expenditures on health and Social Security account for virtually all of the increase in HEW's budget, and these increases are automatic under current law.

**Comment:** I find it difficult to see how we can get the political consensus necessary to spend these large sums for national health insurance until there is some agreement on the goals of our health care delivery system. We can't even really evaluate the costs and benefits of regulations, because they serve so many different goals. My impression is that much of the motivation behind cost containment, particularly in regard to physician fees, is basically social envy. Another goal is redistribution—providing something we think is a middle-class good to disadvantaged folks, whether it's productive or not. "We have it. They ought to have it because it's part of living a decent life." Another goal relates to the public health approach: it is good for the country to have healthier poor people, because not only will they feel better, but they will work better and be happier and more cooperative; there will be less social conflict. That isn't a dominant goal at all. Another goal that is implicitly accepted by many people and explicitly rejected by many others is extending life expectancy. Another one, which to some degree trades off with it, is improving the quality of life without extending life expectancy. Until we sort out all these goals we can't even assess the benefits and costs of the different plans. We're going off in too many directions at once.

**Aaron:** I think the chance of sorting out those questions is nil.

**Question:** Why is that? Why won't they talk it out?

**Comment:** Goal definition is antithetical to building a coalition in order to get something passed in Congress. That's the reason most analysis is done for the executive branch and not for Congress.

**Comment:** I can understand the political process involved in implicitly setting weights on these various goals; I can't understand why there is so little discussion of what those goals are irrespective of their weights. Surely it's obvious that the political process sets these weights and sets the timetable whereby compromises can be made among the different goals and the weights attached to them as they change.

**Aaron:** Some of those goals involve enormously complex reasoning. For example, we don't really know what determines life expectancy; we don't know how to improve it. The quality of life? What does that mean? As far as income distribution is concerned, there are actually a dozen different kinds of redistribution going on. It would be highly unproductive for a person interested in affecting policy to engage in that basic a discussion.

**Comment:** I think that's very realistic. The whole cost containment movement is like somebody trying to plug a hole in a dike under a waterfall. Demand is going to keep growing and costs are going to keep expanding across the board. The essential issue is this expansion of demand and the opportunities to satisfy it. How can we work with mixed public and private systems to provide the most efficient health care services that can meet the level of demand? Demand will continue to expand as more social groups realize that they have a right to equivalent care and as people become educated to the possibilities of living longer and healthier lives. I think it's a very unstrategic allocation of research resources to tamper with some of the bits of machinery within the cost element and try to make them a little more efficient. The effort to contain costs is going to be overwhelmed repeatedly by this continuing acceleration of demand.

**Comment:** The strong desire to have a third-party payment system seems to be driving everything.

**Question:** Doesn't it occur to anyone that the reason people want third-party payments is not necessarily to reduce their apparent out-of-pocket costs, but to assure greater investment in their health care, whether they can afford it or not?

**Comment:** People want an increase in benefits rather than a reduction in costs.

**Comment:**   Martin Feldstein talked for years about maximum liability insurance—essentially catastrophic insurance—and he was well against the tide. Nobody was interested in that kind of plan. People wanted more third-party payments. It was an interesting intellectual aberration within the health analysis community that people focused on third-party payments, which really missed the mark.

**Comment:**   A number of analysts claim that the basic inflationary force is third-party reimbursement, and that the only way to control health care expenditures is to require that beyond some point people pay for health care out of after-tax dollars. This view leads many to stress the efficiency of HMOs. They suggest providing coverage equivalent to HMO health care costs, and beyond that requiring individual payment in after-tax dollars.

**Question:**   If we made automobile insurance illegal, do you think that the accident rate would drop? The implication is that if you have to pay for your problems out of your pocket, you avoid the problems with more diligence.

**Aaron:**   The parallel question is, if we abolish automobile insurance will we reduce the business of automobile repairs? And the answer is yes, without a doubt. As a nation, we have sought third-party payment assiduously. The extension of insurance has been a major part of collective bargaining. Medicare and Medicaid are nothing more than collectively enacted third-party reimbursement. They've been so successful that the solution to yesterday's problem of inadequate financial protection has become today's problem of too few economic constraints.

**Comment:** There seems to be a big difference in terms of emotional response between the first $2,000 of expenditures in catastrophic coverage and other benefits. The trouble is that there is a religious connection between these two tiers of consumption in people's minds, and I don't use the religious analogy frivolously. People have faith in progress, modern science, social responsibility, and family obligations. According to this faith, there is an obligation to expand the first set of costs, before catastrophic illness, in order to avoid the second set of costs. In other words, it is a preventive concept ingrained in us.

**Aaron:** That's right, and the most price-elastic services seem to be the ones that are conventionally called preventive services. If we imposed cost sharing, for example, we would drastically limit preventive dental care.